THE
WEST
INDIES

Islands in the Sun

*Carib Indian stone
marking, St. Vincent Island*

THE
WEST
INDIES

Islands in the Sun

Wilfred Cartey

Montego Bay, Jamaica

Thomas Nelson & Sons

Photographs are from the following sources: Barbados Tourist Board, pp. 25, 71, 85, 181, 209; Caribbean Travel Association, pp. 6–7, 21, 22, 23, 37, 44, 63, 67, 72, 73, 77, 96, 98, 103, 185, 202; Commonwealth of Puerto Rico, Economic Development Administration, pp. 64, 102, 126, 128, 162, 163, 193, 196, 204, 208; Consulate General of Jamaica, pp. 2–3, 31, 48, 60, 78, 116, 121, 124, 137, 146, 176, 182, 190, 205, 210; David Young Studio, pp. 13, 54, 55; Haiti Government Tourist Office, pp. 86, 89; Richard Harrington, pp. 16, 34, 79, 106, 119, 159, 174, 178, 179, 188 (bottom), 191; Pan American Airways, pp. 14, 19, 35, 45, 70, 74, 101, 105, 172, 206, 207; Peace Corps, pp. 92, 93, 112, 127, 134; Walter Rosenblum, pp. 10, 28, 38, 41, 83, 109, 133, 140, 148, 150, 171; Trinidad and Tobago Tourist Board, pp. 18, 51, 56, 57, 113, 143, 167, 187, 188 (top); author's photo, by Gerry Jacobson. Permission is gratefully acknowledged. Permission to quote from the following publications is also acknowledged: Augier, F. R. and Gordon, Shirley C. *Sources of West Indian History* (London: Longmans, Green & Co., Ltd., 1962), pp. 74–75, 84, 86, 88, 90, 175; *Calypsos by the Original Young Brigade* (Trinidad: 1959), pp. 51–52; Campbell, George. *The Kyk-overal Anthology of West Indian Poetry* (British Guiana, 1957), pp. 30–31; Crowley, Daniel J. "Emergence of a West Indian Culture" in *Trinidad Sunday Guardian,* April 20, 1958, p. 30, "The Midnight Robbers," p. 58 and, "The Traditional Masques of Carnival," pp. 57–58, 59, in *Caribbean Quarterly,* Vol. IV, Nos. 3 & 4; Fouché, Franck. *Pages de litterature Haitienne* (Haiti: Imprimerie de l'Etat, 1951), p. 147; Goveia, Elsa. *Aspects of the History of the West Indies* (New Haven: Yale Univ. Press, 1966) pp. 85, 91; Guillén, Nicholás. *El son entero; suma poetica 1929–1946* (Buenos Aires: Editorial Pleamar, 1947), pp. 33, 144–146; Hearne, John. *The Autumn Equinox* (London: Faber, 1959), p. 144, *The Faces of Love* (London: Faber, 1957), pp. 142–143, *Stranger at the Gate* (London: Faber, 1956), pp. 143–144; Lamming, George. *In the Castle of My Skin* (New York: McGraw-Hill, 1953), p. 141; McKay, Claude. *Selected Poems of Claude McKay* (New York: Bookman Associates, 1953), pp. 148–149; Mittelholzer, Edgar. *A Morning at the Office* (London: Hogarth Press, 1950), pp. 32–33; Murray, Tom, ed. *Folk Songs of Jamaica* (London: Oxford Univ. Press, 1951), pp. 48, 49, 50, 180; *Notebook by Macaw* (Trinidad: Trinidad Pub. Co., Ltd., 1960), p. 47; Padilla, Carlos. "Canaveral," p. 147; Roberts, W. Adolphe. *The French in the West Indies* (Indianapolis: Bobbs-Merrill, 1942), p. 80; Springer, H. W. "On Being a West Indian" in *Caribbean Quarterly,* Vol. III, No. 3, pp. 135–136; Williams, Eric. *Documents of West Indian History* (Trinidad: PNM Pub. Co., Ltd., 1963), pp. 63–69, 71, 94.

Published in Camden, N.J., by Thomas Nelson & Sons and simultaneously in Toronto, Canada, by Thomas Nelson & Sons (Canada) Limited.

Design by Harold Leach

Library of Congress Catalog Card Number: 67-13917

Printed in the United States of America

Oh Mother Mine
You who are the Mother of all.

—David Diop

To Ada and to young people of all regions, especially those of the Caribbean Islands

To the many who contributed in the preparation of this book I offer my very sincerest thanks. Sandra Nagel generously helped in the total preparation of the manuscript; with her kindly services and the patient assistance of Susan McNamara, Lucy Colvin, Dorothy Vellenga, Judy Weiner and Marian Leopold the manuscript was finally completed. Together we tripped through history and geography, culture and literature, politics and economics, education and growth of the Islands. To them my warmest gratitude. My thanks also to my research assistant, Eugenia Macer and to those who shared many happy hours of reading—Mrs. Irwin Joseph, Mr. Lewis Gompers of the Lighthouse; to Mrs. William Blake and to Mrs. Robert Carey; and to my friends Helene Aylon, Irene Hochstein, Marian Davis, Jackie Marvel, and Ann Scherck. I would like to express my thanks to Mrs. O'Neil of Recording for the Blind and to that organization for its many services to me; to Dr. Vera Rubin, Director, for opening up to me the valuable resources of the Research Institute for the Study of Man, and to her colleagues Mrs. Jane Lowenthal and Professor Lambrose Comitas for proofreading the galleys, a task for which I must thank also Mrs. Sonia Murray. I should mention the valuable suggestions offered me in the preparation of this book by Professor Elsa V. Goveia of the University of the West Indies. Thanks to Messrs. Lloyd Best and Stuart Hall for their valuable discussion of the project in its early stages.

I have been encouraged in the preparation of this book by several close friends and by my sisters and brothers. I would wish that all of these people mentioned travel with me on my venture through Islands in the Sun.

Wilfred G.O. Cartey

GULF OF
MEXICO

FLORIDA

Miami

Key West

Nassau

BAHAMA ISLANDS

Havana

CUBA

ISLE OF PINES

CAYMAN ISLANDS

Guantanamo

Cap-Haitien

HAITI

Port-au-Prince

Montego Bay

GREATER A

Kingston

JAMAICA

CARIBBEAN L

ARUBA

CURAÇAO

Willemstad

BON.

PANAMA CANAL

SOUTH AMERICA

ATLANTIC

OCEAN

N

W

E

S

THE
WEST INDIES

*Small islands are slightly
enlarged to show detail*

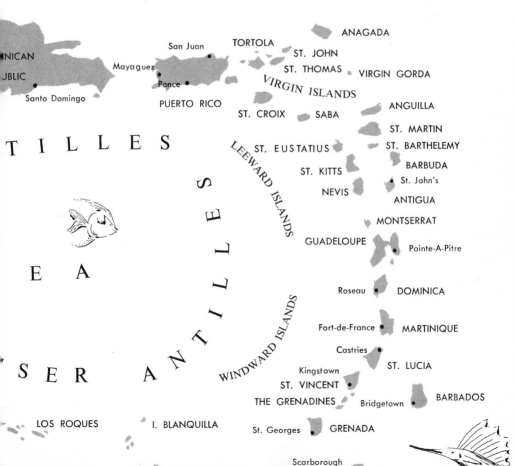

NICAN

JBLIC

Santo Domingo

Mayaguez

Ponce

San Juan

PUERTO RICO

ST. CROIX

ANAGADA

TORTOLA

ST. JOHN

ST. THOMAS   VIRGIN GORDA

VIRGIN ISLANDS

SABA

ANGUILLA

ST. MARTIN

ST. BARTHELEMY

BARBUDA

St. John's

ANTIGUA

T I L L E S

ST. EUSTATIUS

ST. KITTS

NEVIS

LEEWARD ISLANDS

MONTSERRAT

GUADELOUPE   Pointe-A-Pitre

E   A

Roseau   DOMINICA

Fort-de-France   MARTINIQUE

S E R   *A N T I L L E S*

Castries

Kingstown   ST. LUCIA

ST. VINCENT

THE GRENADINES   Bridgetown   BARBADOS

WINDWARD ISLANDS

LOS ROQUES   I. BLANQUILLA

St. Georges   GRENADA

Scarborough

LA TORTUGA   ISLA MARGARITA

Port of Spain   TOBAGO

TRINIDAD

Contents

Foreword   5

Map   6

Islands of Dream   11

One Body—Many Members   29

Centuries of Strife and Settlement   61

The United States in the Caribbean   97

Educating the Community   117

Caribbean Voices   141

Political Unrest and Dependency   157

Economic Life and Prospects   169

Postscript   203

Other Books to Enjoy   213

Highlights in West Indian History   214

Index   217

Islands of Dream

Be not afeard; the isle is full of noises,
Sounds of sweet airs, that give delight, and hurt not.
Sometimes a thousand twangling instruments
Will hum about mine ears; and sometimes voices,
That, if I then had waked after long sleep,
Will make me sleep again; and then, in dreaming,
The clouds methought would open, and show riches
Ready to drop upon me; that, when I waked,
I cried to dream again.
—William Shakespeare, *The Tempest*, Act III, sc. ii.

The islands of the Caribbean make men dream and cast spells over travelers. Christopher Columbus had traveled to new lands in his mind, had dreamed of faraway places and exotic lands, and was not afraid to venture into the unknown.

Was it really unknown? Columbus had heard many tales of the Norsemen's travels in their Viking ships and their discovery of land in the West as well as the tales of Marco Polo's visit to the fabulous court of Kublai Khan in the East. Was it pure fantasy that drove him west to discover eastern lands or did he suspect that the Viking Vinland was the coast or land's end of a region vaster and more remarkable than Polo's kingdom in the East?

Be it fancy or fact, dream or knowledge that motivated him, we know that Columbus eventually persuaded the Spanish monarchs to fit out three ships: the *Niña*, the *Pinta*, and the *Santa María* for a voyage of

A Haitian couple stops to take in the view of the mountains at Plaisance on their way home from market

11

discovery. In persuading the King and Queen of Spain, Columbus, a very religious and devout man, showed that discovery would mean the winning of many new lands and many new converts for the service of God. Being a practical merchant as well, Columbus also foresaw the possibility of vast new areas that would bring new wealth to Spain and power and prestige to him. For he dreamed of having dominion over large regions, and demanded of the monarchs that he be made viceroy over all discovered lands.

Had Columbus discovered what he hoped to—the vast land mass of Asia—he would have ruled over one of the most important areas of the world. He did not discover Asia but islands which, though small in size, were great in historical importance. And, like Caliban's island, the isles of the Caribbean are of wondrous beauty. These are the islands that we, too, shall attempt to discover.

We can reach the islands from Spain in but a few short hours by plane and in less than a week by boat. It took Columbus thirty-six days of anxious sailing before he saw the white cliffs of San Salvador. During the trip he had to pacify the sailors as the ship lay becalmed midst the seaweed of the Sargasso Sea, where the Doldrums robbed the sails of their windpower. Toward the end of the voyage he had to contain the threat of mutiny by his fearful sailors. For, at that time, to sail for thirty-six days without sight of land could tax the patience and strength of the strongest and bravest of men.

Columbus kept two logs of his voyage: one to show to the sailors and one for himself. He shrewdly kept the true distance from the sailors by showing them only the specially prepared log. By so doing he hoped to make them think that they had not traveled as far as they really had. This helped to minimize the danger of mutiny.

Finally, at two o'clock one morning in the year 1492, on the date now celebrated as Columbus Day, a lookout on the *Pinta* cried, "Tierra! Tierra!" The land was the land of the Caribbean Islands. We may imagine the thanks each sailor must have offered to his own special saint. Later that morning, as more of the land became visible, we can also imagine the thrill of the sailors, a thrill the visitor to the islands still feels on first sight of these lands.

12

A plantation worker climbs a tree to harvest coconuts

The Fabric of Dreams

With the words of a Spanish seaman and the sight of the island, the modern history of the lands of the Caribbean began. A merchant's dream had come true. Columbus thought he had reached the Indies. Since he had traveled West, he gave them the name West Indies. The islands have had other names: *Caribbean Islands,* from the name of the sea that girds the islands with its blue waters; *Antilles,* from the name given to the unknown land of geographers of the Middle Ages, the land which lay beyond the sea. Later names would show their changing roles: the *Sugar Islands* they would be called at the height of their prosperity; the *Rum Islands,* after the drink immortalized by Robert Louis Stevenson in his book *Treasure Island;* the *Spice Islands;* and *Islands in the Sun*—for they are luxuriantly sunbathed.

13

Columbus saw the beauty and potential of the islands immediately: the thick foliage, the fertile land with the possibilities for rich harvests, the bright colors and fresh smell which moved him to say: "In all Castile there is no land that can be compared with this for beauty and fertility." The thrill and excitement of his discovery of the islands may be seen from the exaggerated tones of his personal diary:

> . . . there are the mouths of two rivers with the most beautiful champaign country, almost like the lands of Spain. . . . I can never tire my eyes in looking at such lovely vegetation, so different from ours. . . . I found the smell of the trees and flowers so delicious that it seemed the pleasantest thing in the world . . . the mountains and isles . . . so high and clear of clouds and snow, with the sea at their bases so deep. . . . The land is cool and the best that words can describe . . .

In his one letter to the Spanish monarchs Columbus touches upon many elements of the islands and upon many of the possibilities for

Tobago with its palm-fringed beaches is often called Robinson Crusoe's island. Defoe used it as a model for his story of Alexander Selkirk

their development. Although the letter is repetitive and exaggerated in tone, Columbus grasped many of the elements and factors that were to shape the history and growth of these islands. The fertility of the islands is still the main source of their agricultural productivity. The sheltered harbors Columbus noted were used in the sixteenth and seventeenth centuries by Spanish galleons and English, French, and Dutch buccaneers, and now provide one of the essential links in the developing communications network of the islands.

Yet it was not only the exotic beauty of the islands that made them legendary. It was the prospect of finding large quantities of gold that whetted the desires of men and fired their imaginations. The belief in the existence of a Fountain of Youth located somewhere in the newly discovered lands drove generations of men to ever-increasing exploration of the lands around the Caribbean Sea.

Thus the fascination of the islands inspired many writers. Shakespeare set the play *The Tempest* in the Caribbean. It seems to have been inspired by the tales of the adventures of Sir Thomas Gates and Sir George Summer, whose boat was wrecked in the Bermudas during a hurricane in 1609. They had set out in a large fleet for Virginia; however, the *Sea Adventure* was separated from the rest of the fleet by the storm, and it was believed that the ship and its crew had perished. When the men finally reached Virginia the next year, their "return from death" made all the more fascinating the tales of their experiences in the islands.

In the eighteenth century, Daniel Defoe seized upon the chronicle of Alexander Selkirk, who had been set ashore on the island of Juan Fernandez, off the coast of Chile. The captain of the ship which rescued Selkirk, who lived on the island for five years—from 1704 to 1709— published an account of the castaway's adventures. Defoe fashioned this chronicle into the fictional journal of a man who could live alone, finding in nature peace, solace, and companionship, and deriving from nature's bounty everything necessary to life. This is the famous tale of Robinson Crusoe who lived in exotic surroundings on an island modeled after Tobago, which lies off the coast of Trinidad.

15

The dreaded Long John Silver of Robert Louis Stevenson's *Treasure Island,* known to generations for his:

Fifteen men on the Dead Man's Chest—
Yo-ho-ho, and a bottle of rum!
Drink and the devil had done the rest—
Yo-ho-ho, and a bottle of rum!

searched and fought for treasure on an imaginary island re-created from the tales Stevenson heard about the Bahamas.

But Columbus did not "discover" the islands, he opened them to European conquest. The islands already were inhabited by tribes of Indians. The ones he met on his first landing are called Arawaks; they were noted for their peaceful nature. They lived simply, their food consisting mainly of fish from the sea and cassava roots which they dug from the ground. Columbus describes them as "a race of people very poor in everything. . . . They are very well made, with very handsome bodies and very good countenances."

Living in the southern islands were fiercer peoples: the Caribs. The Arawaks and Caribs had both come from northern South America.

This woman is one of the few Carib Indians left on Aruba. A neighboring island, Bonaire, has numerous caves in which ancient Carib drawings are carved in the rock

The Caribs began their northward push about a century before the coming of the Europeans and constantly drove before them the Arawaks, who had lived in the islands for hundreds of years. Columbus named this fierce tribe Caríbals or Caníbals, a word which has come down to modern times as "cannibal," and which describes an activity the Caribs are said to have pursued because of necessity.

All of the Arawaks died either from exploitation and enslavement (overwork in the Spanish mines, for example), from attempted resistance to this exploitation, or as victims of the many new diseases the Europeans brought. The first meeting between Arawaks and Spaniards was symbolic of the destruction to come: "They neither carry nor know anything of arms, for I showed them swords, and they took them by the blade and cut themselves through ignorance."

The Caribs, fiercer and more resilient, suffered a fate little better than that of their gentler brothers. Today, on the mainland of South America, a small number of descendants of the Caribs survive. In the islands, there remain but a handful. The 1960 census indicated 1,265 in St. Vincent, 395 in Dominica, and 150 in St. Lucia.

Not long ago in Trinidad one of the last surviving Caribs, whose birthday had been publicly celebrated for many years, died at the age of more than 100 years. It is sad indeed to witness the disappearance of the first inhabitants of the island. They share a fate with many of the American Indians who could neither physically adjust to nor mentally accept the coming of the Europeans.

Thus the modern history of the islands is the history of the settlement by peoples who came from the Old World. Europeans were the first settlers. Then, with the decimation of the native populations, Africans were brought to work in the mines and plantations. Later, when the descendants of the African slaves were freed, a large number of East Indians from the subcontinent were imported as indentured laborers. Chinese, too, have migrated to the islands.

We see that the islands of the Caribbean are peopled from all over the Old World by a diverse group that has blended together to form a new culture: that of the West Indies.

17

Oriental shops are common-place in Port-of-Spain, Trinidad, one of the most cosmopolitan cities in the West Indies

The Far-flung Antilles

What kind of islands did Columbus reach? Since history and time have not affected the basic geographical features of the area, we experience them in much the same way as did Columbus.

If we were to look at the Caribbean area from the air we would see the islands as several parts of a curve, far-flung and scattered dots sweeping from the southeastern tip of the United States to the northeast coast of South America. It is a curve of some 2,500 miles, and the area from Havana to Trinidad is within the zone of the Tropics.

The largest of the islands is Cuba, with an area of 44,164 square miles —a little larger than the state of Ohio. There are hundreds of islands, most of them quite small, with the smallest of them—in the Florida keys—only an acre or so in size. The islands with significant population range from Cuba with its population of more than 6 million to little Montserrat, in the Leewards, with an area of 33 square miles and a population of about 15,000.

The four largest islands—Cuba, Jamaica, Hispaniola (Haiti and the Dominican Republic), and Puerto Rico—have been given the name *Greater Antilles.* The others are called the *Lesser Antilles.* Within the Lesser Antilles are both geographical and political subgroupings. The

18

former are the Leewards and the Windwards; the latter, the Dutch, French, and British West Indies. Trinidad and Tobago are sometimes included in the Lesser Antilles.

The Windwards and the Leewards are geographical designations for the islands that are directly in the face of the northeast trade winds and those in the lee of the winds. Geographically, this division is said to be at St. Lucia, with the southern islands, to Grenada, called Windwards, and the northern ones, to Anguilla, called Leewards. Administratively, however, the Windwards include Dominica, and the Leewards are only the small northern British islands of Antigua, Montserrat, St. Christopher, Nevis, and Anguilla. Moreover, the Dutch designate their

The beach at St. Lucia with a view of Petit Pitón. The native canoes are dug out of a single tree

northern islands (St. Eustatius, Saba, and the southern part of St. Martin) as Windwards. It is not certain, in fact, whether even the geographical designation corresponds to climatic reality.

The Caribbean Islands stretch from a latitude equal to that of West Palm Beach at about 27° N to a latitude of 10° N in Trinidad. The whole Antilles group lies within the zone of the Tropics. In every respect the islands are tropical: in their vegetation, their climate, their crops, and their way of life. Unlike the large tropical land masses, however, the islands are much influenced by the surrounding sea.

The sea is blue, sparkling water reflecting the blue of the sky. The blue is sometimes shot through with greens of various hues, with rainbow-colored foam in which the sea dolphins and multicolored fish bob up. The waters play around the islands and are driven by the northeast trade winds onto beaches of white or dark gray sand or against cliffs which fall sharply from mountaintops.

Some of the islands have flat coastal regions that slope gently up to small peaks. Barbados and Antigua have long expanses of these flat coastal regions, sloping very gently up to low-lying peaks. Others, like Dominica, rise sharply from a narrow strip of land. The variety is thus apparent: variety of shapes and sizes, of lushness of vegetation, of heights of mountains and hills.

The mountainous islands, with their heavier rainfall and rock soil, have much more luxuriant foliage than the lower limestone and coral islands. The mountaintops are covered, not with snow but with heavy green matted foliage and trees whose arms spread wide from massive trunks.

These mountains rarely rise above 7,000 feet. They are the eastern branches of the mountain chains that stretch through Central and South America. There are essentially two groups which are the result of two prehistoric mountain-building periods. About 100 million years ago at the time the mountains of Mexico and Central America were formed, two branches extended as chains, one to present-day Jamaica, the other through southern Cuba, Hispaniola, and Puerto Rico to the Virgin Islands. At about the same time the Caribbean Coastal Range

20

Mount Pelée in Martinique is one of the few active volcanoes in the West Indies. Sugar cane grows at the foot of the mountain

was formed, stretching through Venezuela, Colombia, Trinidad, and possibly to Barbados. The second group, that of the inner islands of the Lesser Antilles (Saba to Grenada), is the result of mountain-building activity some 75 million years later. These islands were uplifted in a period of building that saw the development of the mountain systems of the Alps, Himalayas, Rockies, and Andes. Some of the older Antillean mountains were affected as well. The last-formed group of islands is a volcanic chain.

Even today some of these volcanoes are still active. In the modern history of the West Indies, some have erupted with tremendous force and devastating fury, pouring their molten lava down the hillsides, the yellow stream cutting a path of death and destruction wherever it flows. Anything in its wake remains fixed forever in a permanent contortion. The ash from these volcanoes, blown by the wind, has traveled hundreds and hundreds of miles.

In 1902, Mt. Pelée in Martinique erupted, destroying the entire town of St. Pierre. Even today the path along which the lava flowed is clearly visible on the side of the mountain.

21

The Rhythms of Weather

The mountains have another important role in the Caribbean. They encourage or prevent rainfall according to their height. The northeast trade winds bear the rain, but the mountains, forcing the winds to rise and thereby to be cooled, produce the rain. Thus, low-lying Barbados has an average rainfall of about 60 inches, and rain here is caused mainly by atmospheric pressure changes. Dominica, which has a mountainous interior, has an average rainfall of about 300 inches a year. Varying heights of the islands produce varying amounts of rainfall. In Jamaica, the yearly average is 77 inches, ranging from about 30 inches in the mid-south to over 100 inches in the northeast. Where island relief is low, of course, other factors produce rain. In the southern Caribbean, for example, it is the arrival and retreat of the rain belt that brings rain.

Winding through tree ferns this road leads up through the dense rain forest of Puerto Rico to El Yunque (The Anvil), the rocky peak at the top

A view of the windward coast of St. Vincent Island showing the black sand which is a distinctive feature of this area

These factors combine to bring about two basic seasons: wet and dry. Some years people call the seasons "rainy and rainier." Lack of a winter and summer means that people need only one wardrobe. They don't need spring coats, winter coats, fall coats, etc., but they do need umbrellas! Rainfall in the Caribbean can be torrential and quick. In fact, within a few seconds you can be soaked through from the large drops that come slanting down from the sky. And just as quickly the rain can stop and the sun come smiling through. It is not unusual for the rain to be falling heavily and the sun to be shining all the while. When this occurs, young people say that "God and the Devil are fighting for a hambone." There is another phenomenon of Caribbean rainfall: it often happens that one side of the street is experiencing torrents of water while the other side is totally dry.

23

Rain affects the punctuality of attendance at school and at work, and very often when it is raining you might easily arrive two hours late without having to give an explanation. Work may be interrupted, but never play! A soccer match will continue and a cricket match will be recessed for the duration of the storm. Not a soul leaves, however.

The same easterly winds that bring rain may develop into hurricanes. Hurricanes are so much a part of Caribbean life that one of the names for the islands is *Hurricane Islands.* Hurricanes commonly form in the areas just east of the French Antilles, to the northeast of Puerto Rico, and in the gulfs of Panama, Yucatan, and Mexico. However, no island is completely safe. Tobago, which is usually out of the path of the summer storms, was "brushed" by Hurricane Flora in 1963. A storm that comes sweeping across the islands can do a tremendous amount of damage, for it may have winds up to 200 miles an hour near its center and often moves as slowly as 10 to 12 miles an hour, or may even remain stationary for a number of hours. A full-blown hurricane may reach 600 miles in diameter.

The destructiveness of these hurricanes is well known in West Indian history, from the three known ones that Columbus weathered, through the 1780 hurricane that destroyed the fleets of three countries and took a toll of 20,000 lives, to Hurricane Flora which hit Cuba in October 1963, killing 1,132 people and damaging from 50 to 100 per cent of Cuba's entire agricultural crop.

When a hurricane is coming, the sky, which always seems so huge in the islands, seems even more immense. Then, too, there is an absence of the white fleecy clouds that ordinarily pile up in the sky and drift lazily across its blue expanse. And now the young people cannot compare the cloud formations to animals and flowers, for the sky is featureless, without contours. It seems hard and heavy. The air, which generally blows from the sea, lightening the heat of the day and making the nights fresh and balmy, is now still. The stillness of the atmosphere brings with it a feeling of danger and of tension. But even more ominous is the way the sun changes very quickly from bright, blood red to black and threatening. On and off the sun seems to turn

24

from red, to black, to yellow. Then people can only wait for the coming of the hurricane.

There is nothing man can do as yet to change the course of the hurricane, which seems to dance lazily on its path of destruction, spinning its winds the way a girl spins her skirts while dancing. All you can do is to pile up your belongings on tables or lash them to the rafters of the house, to batten down the doors and windows, and wait. But you cannot batten down trees and the fruits that hang on them. And when the stillness is broken by strong gusts of wind, which shriek and whistle, the big trees dance and sway wildly in the wind, the fruits scattering far and wide.

This valley in Barbados is protected from hurricanes, but it is difficult to grow crops on the eroded hillsides. In the foreground, a casserina tree grows

In the wake of the hurricanes, driving torrential rains and angry gusty winds bring destruction and death to these lovely islands. But when the rain stops and the winds die down, the anger of the storm may always be forgotten in the beauty of the moon.

. On the mountainous islands the moon comes rising over the peaks to pour its bright blue light straight down into the valley. It is in the valleys where the moonlight of the islands is most beautiful. For instance, the University of the West Indies in Mona, Jamaica, which is ringed in by hills and mountains and which seems to sit at the bottom of a bowl, experiences some of the most beautiful moonlight in the world. So beautiful is the area in the moonlight that songs have been written about it: "Mona Moon!" is well known to all students in the University.

In the flat, low-lying islands where there are few valleys, the moon seems to glow less brightly, but spreads a pale blue light more evenly across the level sands.

But the non-moonlit nights are also beautiful. Then the stars glow by the millions in the sky and pierce the jet blackness of the night. In the black but clear nights, children try to count the stars.

The sun, the moon, the stars, the rain, the sea—all give a rhythm, pattern, and flavor to the islands. Yet all this abundance of natural beauty is not total. The sun at midday blazes down with an intensity that will drive both man and beast to seek the cool shade. Without the convenience of air-conditioning, buildings can become oppressively hot and work becomes more arduous. The sun rises early in the Caribbean. There is not as great a variation in the length of days as in the temperate climates. And yet the sun is not all an enemy, for it helps to ripen the fruits for which the islands are known. It bathes the land with white or yellow light and is sought out by many tourists from the temperate regions. And it gives the islands one of their many names and causes many to sing nostalgically the folk song:

> Oh, islands in the sun,
> Willed to me by my father's hand,
> All my life I will sing in praise
> Of your forest waters and shining sands.

26

These are the "Indies" Columbus discovered, an area that proved to be the gateway to a new world and that saw the development of countries with wealth and power greater than Columbus would ever have dreamed. The West Indies were to play very important roles in the history of that world: as a base for its exploration; as exporter of wealth that enriched the discoverers and later the colonizers of the islands; as the focus for struggles among the European powers and then between some of them and the new giant of the new world, the United States; and later as an area of struggle among the American countries themselves.

This book is the story of these West Indies, the story of their influence on the world, the influence of the rest of the world on the Caribbean and on the diverse peoples who populate the islands, and the present-day result of the interaction of all of these factors.

One Body—Many Members

The peoples who make up the present population of the Caribbean Islands are descendants of people from many regions. They had come from the north and the east; and those who had inhabited the islands before—the Indians—had sailed up from the south. The discoverer Columbus had sailed west to find the East. And after him had come many peoples from Europe—the Spanish, the French, the English, the Dutch, the Danes, the Irish, the Maltese—of all distinctions and of all classes, from the nobleman to the destitute, from the man of religion to the prisoner, all those who sought fortune and abandoned their countries in the search.

People came also from Africa, uprooted and enslaved; they came from various nations and kingdoms, from various tribes and clans. Among them were chieftains and slaves, men learned in African law and those conquered in battle. They came from the banks of the rivers —Gambia or Senegal—or from the grasslands in the interiors: men different, then, from one another through their environment and their background. But people came, too, from farther east, from Lebanon and Syria, from Java, from India and China. The Indians and the Chinese, with their old customs and institutions, were brought as indentured labor.

Uprooted peoples all, they came across the seas to the Islands in the Sun, there to pursue and attempt to maintain their former institutions and cultures, but eventually to merge and to mingle and even in separateness to experience together the histories of the islands and

Many West Indians are descendants of African people who worked as slaves on the great colonial plantations

29

the force that comes from the islands. Their sensibilities were molded by economic exploitation, smallness of the individual islands, the expanses of the sea and the sky, the swell of the tides, and the powers of the hurricanes. Thus in religion, in art, in music, in language, in physical features, in every sphere of man's life, there is mixing in these islands, as races or stocks or clans, brought together in the narrow confines of an island, commingle. So there is diversity and yet there is an amazing homogeneity. The islands, whose intercommunications were limited for many centuries and are still limited now, in their essences have remarkable similarities. Here we will try to show how diverse, yet how together, in feeling and mood and tone, are the Caribbean islands in the sun. Daniel J. Crowley, in an article in the *Trinidad Sunday Guardian,* April 20, 1958, says:

> West Indians are perhaps more conscious of their cultural debts than any other nation on earth for the very good reasons that they have borrowed so widely and so recently, and that as a result many of the cultural sources are still apparent.

Indeed, if you traveled down the islands, you might be startled by the variety of faces and complexions, of physical types and admixtures, of religions and rituals. You would be amazed, too, if you were to search carefully, at the variants in language and speech patterns, the quantity of folk tales, folklore and folk beliefs, the vitality and rhythmical power of the different songs and dances. You would see, too, the range of architectural forms, from the great houses to the huts and shacks, from the newly constructed hotels to the old forts and historical mansions. Peoples are diverse and yet the same, for they have suffered the same history; their various heads seem to George Campbell a thing of worship as he says in his poem, "Holy":

> Holy be the white head of a Negro
> Sacred be the black flax of a black child.
> Holy be
> The golden down
> That will stream in the waves of the winds
> And will thin like dispersing cloud.

Holy be
Heads of Chinese hair
Sea calm sea impersonal
Deep flowering of the mellow and traditional.
Heads of peoples fair
Bright shimmering from the riches of their species;
Heads of Indians
With feeling of distance and space and dusk;
Heads of wheaten gold,
Heads of peoples dark
So strong so original:
All of the earth and the sun!

31

And if the heads are different, the features of the various peoples comprising this *pot pourri* of races are also distinctive. The West Indian novelist, Edgar Mittelholzer, in his novel *A Morning at the Office*, brings together people of various races—the Negro, the East Indian, the mixed mulatto girl, the white, the Chinese. For instance, here is a picture of the office boy Horace:

> He was a negro nineteen years old, five feet nine and thick-set in build, with broad shoulders. Swimming and weight-lifting had toughened his physique and given him well-developed arm muscles. Of a dark brown complexion, he kept his hair cut close to the skull so that when he had just come from the barber his skull gleamed like bronze and resembled a work of superior sculpture, for it was a well-shaped skull. For a negro, he had remarkably low cheekbones. His forehead was wide and domed; his eyebrows thick and frowning—again, remarkably so for a negro. He had a strong, firm chin.

And here is the contrast between Horace and the chief stenographer, Mrs. Hinckson:

> . . . he was only a black boy, whereas she was a coloured lady of good family. His complexion was dark brown; hers was pale olive. His hair was kinky; hers was full of large waves and gleaming. He was a poor boy with hardly any education, the son of a cook; she was well off and of good education and good breeding. He was low-class; she was middle-class.

Or here again, a physical description of Mr. Jagabir:

> A dark Indian, handsome and with thick, black hair brushed back from his forehead in a high, domed mass, and thick, black eyebrows. . . . He had pale brown eyes which, against his dark brown complexion, constituted his most noteworthy feature.

And finally, Mr. Reynolds, a mixture of races and peoples:

> Mr. Reynolds' French and English ancestors were responsible for his dead-straight hair, and his negro ancestors for the nose which was small and bridgeless with wide nostrils. Though taken with the

32

rest of his face—light brown eyes, small, thin-lipped mouth and low cheekbones—it did not seem an obviously negroid nose.

In certain lights, Mr. Reynolds could have passed for pure white, especially as a faint pinkness sometimes showed under his sallow complexion. . . .

All of these people live side by side, and move and mingle together in the Caribbean Islands. In one person is the grandfather of Spanish stock mixed with the grandfather of African blood, both perpetuating their characteristics and customs in him. And the Cuban poet Nicolás Guillén says:

Shadows that only I see,
Shadows of my two grandfathers who live in me.

Lance with a point of bone,
Drum of skin and wood:
There my black grandfather.
Ruffs on his slender neck,
Grey breastplate for war:
There my white grandfather.

Or, in the English-speaking islands, the poet Derek Walcott, in "A Far Cry from Africa," is torn between his two heritages, the English and the African:

I who am poisoned with the blood of both,
Where shall I turn, divided to the vein?
I who have cursed
The drunken officer of British rule, how choose
Between this Africa and the English tongue I love?
Betray them both, or give back what they give?
How can I face such slaughter and be cool?
How can I turn from Africa and live?

The poet, with his artist's sensibility, is torn between two races; yet the peoples of the Caribbean, thrown together haphazardly by history, are knit together by the islands. For there is a sensibility common to the peoples of the Caribbean Islands, there is a feeling and tone and

33

mood generated by the islands and the seas around the islands. If you went to the islands, you would see the various ingredients of the peoples who have been fused together there. The various races and nations have contributed to the total formation of the present-day Caribbean.

Heritage

It is hard to imagine the Caribbean Islands without the African element in them. The African slaves had brought their religion and music, their customs and foods (such as *callalu, pemi, accra*), their national dances and calypsos, proverbs and Anancy stories, and many other things we will discuss later. The Asians came, also as laborers; the first Indians arrived in the islands in 1845 and the Chinese began coming, some say as early as 1806, while others say 1853. They each brought their festivals and foods: Indian curry, *roti, dhalpurri,* chutney; Chinese *pow choy* and *wun yee,* pork with *foo chook* and *kim chim.* And the Indians brought the Hindu Ramleela and Hosein festivals, along with such religious customs as the red, white, and green flags that fly in Hindu yards as a tribute to Hanuman, the Monkey God. The Europeans came, with their languages and educational systems, legal and

This priest of Hindu origin is about to blow on a conch shell calling his people to prayer. His tiny temple is a few miles outside Port-of-Spain, Trinidad

About one third of Trinidad's population is from the Orient, and many mosques and temples give an exotic touch to the skyline

governmental forms, their sports and dances and music. But, as we know, before the coming of the Europeans, the islands had been peopled by Indian tribes, the Arawaks and the Caribs. We know, too, that their lot was a tragic one; and now little remains to remind us of the earliest settlers of these islands: cassava, some pottery and basketry, the *pirogue* (a small canoe in which they sailed from island to island), and two things that have contributed much to man's comfort, and perhaps to his decay—the hammock and tobacco.

There are a few Indian place names, such as Chacachacare, Guayaguayare, Tamana, Arima; and there are traces of the old Carib dances in the *plena* music of Puerto Rico. Here and there throughout the

35

islands are memorials attesting to the existence of the first inhabitants. In Curaçao, for instance, there are many caves in which can be found drawings done by the Caribs. And so we say that their influence in the formation of the present-day Caribbean peoples was small.

On one or two islands live little groups, last remnants of a dying race. On the mountainous island of Dominica, on a reservation set aside for the Carib Indians, stands the village of Bataka. Its 200 people live in small wooden houses among fruit trees, connected by footpaths leading also to their vegetable gardens, to the forest where they gather food, and to the beach from which they launch their fishing boats. The Caribs, like the Maroons of Jamaica, lead an isolated life because Bataka lies in one of the most inaccessible parts of Dominica. They are self-sufficient, having little economic contact beyond the village, except when young men cross the sea illegally to work in the neighboring French island of Guadeloupe, where they save their earnings to return to Bataka. Although they gave up their own language at the end of the nineteenth century for the Creole patois of Dominica and they now live much the same as their Creole neighbors do, still the Caribs, with their light skin and straight hair, are aware of their racial and cultural distinctiveness and remain a small, inbred community.

Also living in isolation, and divorced from much contact with other peoples, is a group of white settlers on the small Dutch island of Saba. Their forebears arrived some 300 years ago and now the small handful of whites, who yet constitute the most numerous group on the island, live to themselves, apart from the other inhabitants. They make a precarious living from agriculture, but those who leave always want to return to their island.

Beliefs and Rituals

There are few isolated and insulated groups such as these two in the Caribbean Islands. For in these islands, where people have mingled, institutions also have blended together and borrowed from one another. For example, African ritual worship and belief, which continued in the Caribbean Islands, borrowed from Roman Catholic ritual and

36

ceremony, and the blend produced New World forms of African ritual. Many religions of the world have come to the Caribbean and are observed by the peoples of these islands. With the Spaniards and French came Roman Catholicism, which now has many, many adherents in the islands. To be sure, Roman Catholicism is strongest in the islands where the Spaniards and French settled longest and where Spanish and French are spoken. It is, or was, the main religion of Cuba; it is the main religion of Puerto Rico, the Dominican Republic, Haiti, Martinique, Guadeloupe, and some of the English- and patois-speaking islands, such as Dominica and St. Lucia.

The Roman Catholic church early attempted to exclude Jews and Muslims from the islands, and many decrees to that effect were issued from Spain. Yet Jews did come; and now in many islands, their synagogues lend another element to the blended architecture of the Caribbean. For instance, in 1651, some Portuguese Jews came from Brazil to Curaçao, where under a liberal charter, which granted them free-

A Catholic church at Pointe-à-Pitre on the French island of Guadaloupe

Worshippers throng to a religious festival at Saut d'Eau, Haiti

dom of religion, they soon founded a congregation, using a plantation building for a synagogue. A few years later they were joined by Jews from Holland, who went into trade and business. By 1692, a synagogue was built in Willemstad by the wealthy and powerful Jewish community, which still today holds an important position in Curaçao's economy.

The French and the Spanish attempted to prohibit Protestant worship in their islands and allowed public office only to Catholics. The English at first established the Anglican church wherever they settled, treating their Caribbean possessions as part of the diocese of London. Today the Anglican religion is widely practiced in Jamaica, Barbados, Trinidad, and other islands where English systems prevail.

The Quakers also came to the islands and, before any other religious group there, they demanded the repeal of slavery. Other sects came and established congregations, including Moravians, English Baptists, Methodists, Congregationalists, Scotch Presbyterians, Lutherans, the Church of God, the Brethren, Jehovah's Witnesses, Seventh Day Adventists. And so now in the islands all these forms of Christian worship are practiced by the religious.

But in the majority these are European religious institutions. The islands also are full of African rituals and ceremonies and worship services that very often have a pantheon of African gods with corresponding Christian—especially Roman Catholic—saints. These rituals are sometimes outlawed, but they are still observed by quite a number of people who may be *both* members of one of the established churches and followers of these religious groups. It is not wrong to say that the majority of the followers are the poor people, even though the rich and better educated sometimes fall back upon these beliefs when more "civilized" remedies fail to solve some problem.

Let us follow some of these beliefs, the ceremonies accompanying them, the music and drums guiding them, the ritual objects that are symbols of the belief, the spirits and gods who answer the call of the believers. For instance, in Jamaica there is a religious group, Cumina, whose very name shows its West African origin; it comes from the common West African name "kwamena." The Cumina followers worship spirits to whom they give the name "zombies." They believe that their gods came originally from Africa, and they trace their families back to links with gods of the Ibo, Yoruba, and Mandingo people. There are sky gods, who are the mightiest of the gods, with such resonant names as Ofo, Belgium, Abrack, Flash, Abeegil; there are powerful earth-bound gods, too: David, Mabell, Moses, King Makoo, Archie, Obe.

During the ceremony, the people believe that many of these gods breathe their spirits into the bodies of worshipers, so that a man or woman becomes possessed of the spirit and dances. The gods come to the ceremony in response to the songs and slow dances and drum-beats of the people. When a god decides to come, he enters the dancing tent down the center pole and passes through a basin of water and through the ground to a drummer. As the drummer feels the spirit he quickens his tempo, the dancers move faster and faster, and the god moves through the ground to his chosen worshiper. The god enters the worshiper's feet and the feet seem riveted to the ground; and as the god moves up the worshiper's body, the different parts of the body begin to vibrate until the god reaches the shoulders or head, when the worshiper, completely possessed, describes in extraordinary dance patterns the particular dance of his god. As the god came, so he leaves: from head to shoulders, down to feet, into the ground, and out and away through the center pole. Many of the gods dance by possessing a human body in this way, but the most frequent dancers are the ancestral zombies, the spirits of dead members who danced in possession when they lived and who now guard the congregation against evil spirits. These ancestral zombies are called by their human names: William Bailey, Archie Pierce, Amilia Miller.

This is but one part of the ceremony of Cumina, which is only one of the many religious cults in the Caribbean Islands. For instance, in Trinidad there are Shango and Shouters; in St. Vincent there is Rada; in Martinique, Maldevidan; in Haiti, Vodun; in Cuba, Santeria; in Jamaica, Revivalism and Pocomania. All of these cults have points of resemblance; all have combined Christian forms of worship with African or Hindu patterns of ceremony. Yet all have their own distinct patterns.

Some Revivalists draw their saints from the Old and New Testaments of the Bible. Thus God, the Holy Spirit, the archangels Michael and Gabriel, the prophets, such as Elijah and Daniel, all these come to possess the worshipers and to dance at Revivalist ceremonies. The four evangelists live in the corner posts of the "dancing booth" and enter it down the center pole. Also the spirits of the dead, both good and evil, return: the leaders (shepherds and shepherdesses) of past ceremonies return in spirit; but also "duppies" may come, perhaps disguised as snakes, frogs, or lizards. These duppies are one of the two souls that the people believe every human being has; when a person dies, one of his souls goes to God for judgment, but the other, the duppy, remains on earth. Unless it is put to rest by the proper

40

Interior of a voodoo temple in Haiti where African gods are still worshipped in the villages and even in the cities. A suppliant kneels before the candles in a ritual combining Christian and pagan rites

ritual after death, the duppy may wander and cause trouble among the congregation.

This belief that one person has two souls is found also in many West African religions. Other African elements in Caribbean cults include the belief in many gods, who play a direct part in the lives of people; the return of the spirits of the dead; possession of worshipers by the gods and spirits; the rhythm of the drumming, singing, and dancing; the sacrifice of a fowl or goat. Along with these African concepts, European elements enter the ceremonies: the singing of psalms and hymns; the burning of incense and candles; the use of shepherd's crooks and crosses. The African and European blend and merge in these Caribbean cults: the Bible may be used as a charm against duppies; a Christian saint may take on the qualities of an African god.

Also, in Haiti, where many people are both Roman Catholics and believers in the religious cult Vodun, Christian saints and African gods come together. For instance, there is a Vodun god, Damballa, named after the serpent god of Dahomey. The people identify him with St. Patrick, because on the little colored pictures given out by Roman Catholic priests, St. Patrick is shown holding snakes. And Moses is known as the "father of Damballa" because of the Old Testament story in which Moses turned a staff to a serpent before the eyes of the Egyptians. Similarly, worshipers of Vodun sometimes identify St. Peter with Legba, the god who guards crossroads and temple entrances in Dahomey, just as Peter is supposed to guard the gates of the Christian heaven. In Cuba, however, St. Peter is equated with Ogun, the powerful Yoruba god of iron and of war. In Trinidad, the followers of Shango compare St. Peter to the Yoruba fisherman god Ebejee, while Ogun, with his warlike character, becomes St. Michael. Shango himself, the god of lightning and of thunder, is thought to be St. John the Baptist; and Osain, the herbalist god of the jungle is St. Francis.

But at times Christian beliefs are found mingled with Hindu practices. The East Indian cult of Maldevidan in Martinique is an example of this mixing. The chief god is Maldevidan, represented as a man on horseback and identified with Christ. And Mari-eman, the principal female god, has similarities to both the Christian Virgin (Marie Aimée) and the Hindu goddess Mother Mari (Mari-amma). The worshipers hold ceremonies, which they call "masses," on Sundays during the harvest season. During the mass, the leader (*l'abbé coolie*) becomes possessed of the spirit; he dances, slashing the air with machetes, and then stands barefoot on the machete blade while he proclaims the god's words. After this, he sacrifices a fowl, beheading it with a single blow of the same machete; and the congregation joins in a feast. And so we see that the religions and rituals and ceremonies and beliefs of the many peoples who came to the Caribbean all live on in some fashion and, merged together, form a part of the amazing diversity and equally amazing uniformity of the islands.

Beyond Belief

This whole complex of religion brings with it a certain amount of superstition because, when they meet an unexplainable occurrence, people turn to superstition, which extends into folklore. Folklore and its folk tales are told in the folk languages, of which there are many in the Caribbean. For instance, the names of many creatures in Caribbean myths and stories may be French in origin: Papa Bois (or Daddy "Bouchou") is a spirit of the forest, a fierce and strong old Negro man whose very name frightens children. Papa Bois is a protector of animals and he uses his swift feet and keen mind to outrun and outwit the hunters who try to harm the animals.

La Diablesse ("Jablesse") lies in wait for young people who are returning late from parties and dances. She lures them away from the road and then vanishes, leaving them lost in the woods. Everyone fears her; and anyone who sees her makes a sign of the cross on the ground for protection.

The Douennes are the spirits of little children who died before they were baptized; West Indian parents keep children quiet at night by telling them that if they make noise, the Douennes will take away their voices and lead them far from home to the forest.

Soucouyants are wicked spirits who suck human blood. During the

43

A typically French fountain marks the town center at Fort-de-France, Martinique

day they appear as normal human beings, but at night they shed their human skin and take on spirit form, possibly a ball of fire. They can be trapped by salting their human skin, which then shrinks so they cannot get it back on.

Lagahoos are even more various in form; they range from tiny to huge creatures, and they frighten people who have stayed out late at night, trying to follow them into their houses.

44

A Blend of Tongues

Not only are there French names in Caribbean folklore; many folk tales are also told in a form of French. Here is a typical beginning of a Haitian folk tale:

> Té gô fâm ki té gé twa pitit.

> (Il y avait une femme qui avait trois enfants;
> there once was a woman who had three children)

The language here is Creole, which has evolved from French. It includes archaic French forms as well as a basic French vocabulary; to these have been added Indian words for local flowers, fruits, and animals; African terms for religious beliefs, foods, household objects, as well as the African tendency toward repetition for emphasis and the imitation of sounds associated with the thing designated; and also a bit of Spanish from the Dominican Republic and Cuba, and some English from the time of the American occupation. It is said that in St. Lucia,

A Creole woman sells handmade brooms before her shop in Martinique. Her dress is that of a plantation worker during the French colonial period

probably 80 per cent of the children speak a French Creole patois in their homes. (Patois is a dialect used in a particular area and based on the language spoken in that area.) In Dominica, Martinique, and Guadeloupe many people also speak a kind of French patois. But Haiti is the only Caribbean country where a new, hybrid language is spoken by the whole population. The many peasants of Haiti (about 90 per cent of the population) speak only Creole. It is the language in which the upper-class Haitians feel most at home, in spite of the fact that they can speak "proper" French as well as the best-educated Frenchmen. There is a Creole expression:

C'est Créole m'ap palé avé-ou, oui.

(Listen, it's Creole I'm talking to you.)

This saying is used when an upper-class official, or any other Haitian, pretends not to understand what is being said to him. Creole is being written more and more now, and being systematized to the extent where there are not only folk tales but also novels and poetry written in this language. And one of the most beautiful Caribbean songs, "Choucoune" (known elsewhere as "Yellow Bird"), is sung now only in Creole rather than the French in which it was written in the early nineteenth century.

Even as racial strains have mixed and religions have fused, languages have blended together in the Caribbean to produce a variety of patois. English, French, Spanish, and Dutch are the official languages; yet in one small area, at least three of these languages may have been spoken at one time or another, and you can find people, animals, streets, and other places whose names originate in all three languages. The blend of all these languages with African and Indian elements produces an amazing mosaic of speech patterns, each with its distinctive variations of stress, pitch, rhythm. Even when the basic language is the same, the dialect varies from island to island. For instance, the English dialect in Jamaica differs from that in Trinidad, which again is different from that of Barbados. In Curaçao and Aruba you can hear English, Spanish, and Dutch spoken with many accents. You can also hear Papiamento, which combines Indian, African, Spanish, Portuguese, Dutch, English, and French words. In Trinidad, some of the older folk speak a patois of French origin, and in some areas, an old Spanish patois. Some of the older East Indian people speak Hindi or Urdu; and now even some of the younger East Indians are learning it in school. You can hear, too, Cantonese spoken in the streets of Trinidad, and Hebrew, and an English dialect which is called Trinidadian. In the following story, "The Lie," from *Notebook by Macaw,* the boys speak Trinidadian:

> Poor Cyril. He has had to break his engagement to one of the nicest girls in town. And he is taking it badly.
> He moaned to his pals:
> "Boy, woman is France, yes! Dey tell you dey love you, but dey doesn't mean it, nuh, true. You hear what happen to me?"
> The boys said that half of Port-of-Spain had heard.
> "Well, you ever hear t'ing so? Buh she is the onliest woman I ever love dat is why ah tell she to keep the engagement ring. I feel dat I doan want to engage nobody again."
> The boys sympathised and tried to console him with the thought that it was not impossible that she would telephone him tomorrow and all would be well again.
> Cyril looked doubtful: "Ah doan t'ink so, nuh. She doan even want mih to pass by she house. And all because she catch mih in one little lie, yes."
> "One lie?"
> "Yes, because she fine out ah married, she break de engagement. Dat is anything to break up engagement for?"

The humor shown in this story is characteristic of a certain bantering attitude that often seems to pervade Caribbean speech and life. The people of the Caribbean seem to have an ability to laugh at one another and at themselves; and speech often has two levels to it. On the surface, what a person says may seem quite serious, but underneath, there is a deep chuckle. This teasing language appears in many songs of the Caribbean. It appears in the Cuban guarachas, the Jamaican mentos, or the Trinidadian calypsos. For instance, here is a verse from a Jamaican mento, "Nobody's Business," in which a woman tries to ward off prying eyes:

> Solomon granpa gawn a Equador,
> Lef him wife an' pickney outa door,
> Nobody's bus'ness but him own.
> Solomon gramma swear she naw go beg,
> Tief weh all bra Sammy fowl an' egg,
> Nobody's bus'ness but she own.

This is but one of the many songs in the Caribbean, for indeed the isles "are full of noises, sounds of sweet airs that give delight, and hurt not."

Prince Buster (in cap), one of the leading exponents of the Jamaican ska, does one of the new steps in the street before his record shop in Kingston

Many Melodies, Many Rhythms

As in religion and in language, so too in music, dance, and song the various strains that met and merged in the Caribbean have produced an exciting variety of music, rich in melodies and resonant with rhythms. The songs are both religious and secular; some have added African overtones to European music and words; many have the full sap of Africa, blended with Latin American and European flavors. There are Christian or semi-Christian hymns; and there are the ritual songs harking back to African rhythms and even African words. There are work songs that men sing at labor or at rest at the end of a day. At times, the day is long and they yearn for home: "Day dah light an' me wan' go home," as expressed in the Banana Loaders' Song. Island people work on sea as well as on land, so the Jamaicans and Barbadians still sing sea chanties as did the British sailors of many years ago.

In Tobago and many islands of the eastern Caribbean, the older folk in the villages still dance the reels and quadrilles that came with the first European settlers; but the words accompanying these dances tell of life in the Caribbean today. You can see polkas and mazurkas in Trinidad and the French West Indies, and the old Spanish *seis* in Puerto Rico. The older people dance the castiliane, too; in Trinidad, for instance, it is wonderful to see the older folk, who had been sitting quietly while the young folk danced, suddenly spring to life at the call of the castiliane music. They spin and turn and mark with vigorous stamping a three-beat pause that breaks up this very fast waltz. Then even the best young dancer cannot outclass them. For one dance, the whole floor is left to the whirling and twirling of the old. The young urge them on with loud clapping and cheering. Finally, exhausted but smiling happily, the old folk sit down again quietly. The young continue, dancing to the beat of Cuban rhumbas, Haitian and Dominican merengues, Martiniquan beguines, and Trinidadian calypsos.

It is perhaps in music that the islands find their closest unity. All through the Caribbean there are lullabies to quiet the children at night and game songs that enliven their days. "Hol' Yuh Han' " is an example

49

of a game song in which boys and girls dance together in a large circle, "flirting" and dancing out the song.

Dis long time gal me never see you,
Come meck me hol' yuh han'.
Peel-head John Crow sidung pon tree top
Pick off de blossom.
   Meck me hol' yuh han', gal,
   Meck me hol' yuh han'.
Meck we weel and tun till we tumble dung,
Meck me hol' yuh han', gal.

Then there are folk songs and dances that form the basis of some popular music: the beguine in Martinique and Guadeloupe fused African and French folk music. Nowadays, although they retain their folk flavor, beguines are composed for particular occasions, with words referring to current topics. In Puerto Rico there is the popular music of the danza and the plena, bringing together Spanish and African strains to animate and enliven Puerto Rican parties and dances. The Haitian and Dominican merengues, the Cuban rhumbas, the Jamaican and Trinidadian calypsos, are known in most parts of the world. And the limbo, a dance from the Caribbean, adds gaiety and excitement to parties in London, New York, Chicago, Accra, in fact, in most parts of the world.

Perhaps one of the greatest achievements of Caribbean music is the combination of the calypso and the steel band. The calypso derives from *kalinda,* the stick-fighting song the African slaves brought with them from the Guinea coast. The song was sung on the sugar plantations to mark Canboulay, the time of the burning of the cane. Today calypso is sung at all times. It is a very spontaneous creation that comments, often satirically, on political, social, and economic happenings. The Calypsonians, who create these songs, give themselves many grand titles; for instance, there is Lord Kitchener, Lord Invader, Caruso, Lord Melody, and the Mighty Sparrow. They poke fun at any and every thing. No one is so elevated that he cannot be ridiculed, and no event so internationally significant that it cannot be sung in calypso. Here,

50

A group of West Indians dance the limbo, a Caribbean dance which has become internationally famous

for instance, Sparrow comments on United States space efforts in "Explorer,"

> Where did explorer go?
> Nobody know.
> Some think it's in space;
> They can't find a trace
> Because when they let it go
> They forgot to switch on the radio.
>
> Now they think it fell in the ocean,
> They think it fell in the sea.
> But I don't care where it fall as long as it
>   ain't fall on me.
> Explorer, Explorer, somebody made a mistake at
>   the controls and send it out of this world.

51

And here, in more earthy vein, Sparrow gives his opinion on ladies' fashions in "The Sack":

> She must be insane;
> Florence but a chemise again.
> Well this one make it twenty-two.
> Ah don't know what she mean to do,
> But ah sure if she buy one more
> Ah go take dem and wipe the floor.

Some Folk Festivals

Calypsos are sung at any time of the year, but are chiefly composed for Trinidad's gayest, most colorful and most artistic festival, Carnival. Many of the islands have festivals. In Jamaica, Christmas Day marks the start of John Canoe in the rural areas. John Canoe commemorates that time in the old days when the African slaves took advantage of the relaxed Christmas spirit to dress up and mimic their masters. Today the festival retains the haunting African music of drums and flutes and the grotesque gestures of the dance. The dancers wear masks representing such creatures as Horsehead, Cowhead, the Devil, and John himself, with his canoe-shaped headgear. On Christmas Day, these characters dance to the main square of the district and then move on to the surrounding houses where they may receive food and drink or money. During the following week the whole village dances in the evenings, winding up the holiday season with a grand all-day dance on New Year's Day.

The East Indians of Trinidad have brought festivals from India and have added to them elements from the Creole culture of their new home. The Hindu festival Ramleela centers on a dramatic performance of the Hindu epic poem, the *Ramayana.* For ten consecutive days young men act out the elaborate drama; but in Trinidad the actors may be Muslim or Christian as well as Hindu, so long as they follow the order to eat no meat during the time of the festival. They dress in costumes and dance to drumming that has taken on a West Indian quality.

About the same time as Ramleela, the Muslims hold their festival of

Hosein. In commemoration of the death of a great leader, grandson of Mohammed, his followers build a *tadjah*. This is an elaborate, brightly colored paper temple, richly decorated with minarets, pillars, domes, rosettes, flags; it can be as high as twenty-five feet. At night, the East Indians gather, wearing their dhotis and saris; and the chief male celebrants dress in costumes and "dance the moon." These moons, semicircular and measuring as much as eight feet across, are made on a base of metal or wood. This frame is covered with colored paper of various shades and decorated with sequins, beads, and bells, which tinkle as the dancers whirl about dextrously balancing the heavy moons on their shoulders. Many people of African descent join in the festivities. People of all complexions mill about in crowds, eating the Indian foods that are being sold at almost every street corner and generally enjoying themselves during the three to seven days before the festival concludes by pushing the *tadjah* into the sea.

Carnival in Trinidad

The festival of Carnival is celebrated in most of the Caribbean Islands which had been settled by the French or Spanish, but Carnival in Trinidad excels them all. Here, perhaps more than anywhere else, we see the amazing coming together of cultures from all parts of the world. The name Carnival means "goodbye to flesh"; and the festival, which takes place on the two days before the Christian Lenten season, offers the last chance for mad abandonment and festivities. The celebration also coincides with the harvesting and cane-burning season. During this time of Canboulay, the African slaves were allowed a brief relaxation after the hard work of harvesting. And, as with John Canoe, the slaves celebrated by mocking their masters in song, dance, and pantomime. To this day Trinidadians who dress up for Carnival say that they are going to "play ol' mas'."

The songs giving verve and spirit to Carnival are of the Caribbean, even though their rhythms resemble those of West African high life and Latin American music. The steel-band music to which the people dance and "jump up" in the streets for many days, was born in the

53

A Carnival group in costume, with the man on the right impersonating an old dandy. Street-dancing goes on day and night for two days in Trinidad

Caribbean, in Trinidad. It is perhaps the most rhythmical and compelling of music. Before it, much of the music for Canboulay and Carnival was provided by tamboo bamboo (tamboo perhaps from the French *tambour*—drum, and bamboo from the island), whose music came from the beating of bamboo sticks together or on the ground. From this grew the steel band, which in its beginnings replaced the bamboo stems with pieces of steel that were struck together to produce a sharp, clanging, driving rhythm. To this was added music beaten from ordinary dustbins and oildrums, of which there are many on the oil-producing island of Trinidad. Eventually these steel drums were tuned by pounding with hammers to make sections concave or convex; and from this a whole range of musical tones could be summoned by round rubber heads at the end of sticks of wood. There is a whole variety of drums, from the big ones giving bass rhythm to the small ones producing the sweet tenor notes. It is difficult to hear this music and sit still; the feet move, the body shifts, the pulses quicken as the vibrations from the music reach out. The rhythms are urgent and demand movement.

And such movement takes place during the Carnival season. For many weeks before the two days of dancing in the streets, preparations for

Grotesque masks, as well as colorful costumes, are an important part of Carnival

its celebration are under way. The island hums with activity as "bands" prepare their costumes and Calypsonians compose and sing their songs in calypso tents, vying for the title of "King Calypso." For it is the best calypso that will resound throughout the island on the drums of the steel bands. The best calypso is called the "Road March"; but at Carnival time there is no marching on the roads; there is only wild, happy dancing. Indeed, the isle is full of music at this time; there is music in yards and in hills, in valleys and plains, in villages and cities.

As early as Christmas, people begin forming groups called "bands" to participate in Carnival. A theme is chosen by each group, costumes are designed and made, and the group members prepare their Carnival "act." Trinidadians of today have retained much of the mocking spirit of their ancestors; so in the Carnival bands they poke fun not only at the mighty but at all the many types of people who touch on the life of this cosmopolitan island, and also at the human condition in general. One of the most popular themes for the bands is sailors on bad be-

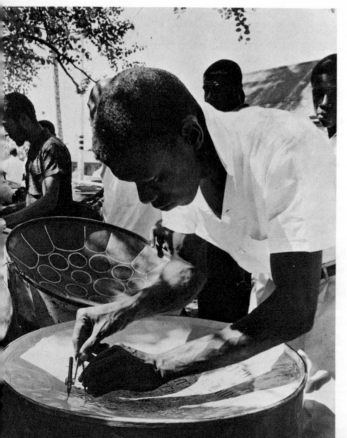

Steel drums are tuned by marking out definite areas on the top of an oildrum, then tempering them to play different notes

havior, as described by Daniel J. Crowley in "The Traditional Masques of Carnival":

> Bad behaviour sailors traditionally walk on their heels, with their hands held in front, fingers spread, and with a rolling gait. When walking alone they mimic drunkards, lurching diagonally right and left and dragging their feet. Variations of staggering are added to this basic form, plus pirouetting and occasional short dance steps or somersaults or other tumbling. A few sailors together may try more elaborate tumbling, balancing acts, and every kind of hi-jinks with the spectators, particularly leering at young girls and making "fatigues," witty conversational asides. En masse the bad behaviour sailors walk six or eight abreast with arms around each others' shoulders. The line thus formed moves three or four steps diagonally right, then three or four steps diagonally left, giving a

convincing performance of drunken sailors which is locally termed "rocking the ship." Alternate lines move in opposite directions, so that in the usual sailor band of from 200 to 800, the street becomes a mass of relatively-patterned movement. The effect is sometimes heightened by the singing or whistling of such Navy songs as "Anchors Aweigh" to the accompaniment of a steel band.

More playful than the sailor bands are the devil bands, which impersonate creatures of the underworld, some looking like bats, others like Lucifer, with horns and tail and spear. Clowns dance among the bands, and robbers roam in bands or as individual "midnight robbers." The midnight robber appears in various disguises—cowboy, hunter, crusader, Viking—and he gives himself some grandiose name such as the Black Prince, King Agag, Rollo de Ganja, Turban Kelly, the Braggeling Ghost. His essential equipment, besides a mask and costume, is a whistle to draw the attention of the victim, a weapon to brandish at him, a sack in which to stow his loot, and a long, elaborate speech which threatens the victim while boasting of the robber's past exploits. The speech is intended to persuade the victim to contribute something to the robber's sack. Here, for example, from Daniel J. Crowley's "The Midnight Robbers," is part of a robber's exaggerated speech in which he describes his escape "from the great jail of Alcatraz":

> "I then landed in Oklahoma. My name was then known to Scotland Yard. Placards of my photograph and fingerprints were posted in each business place . . . but that was not satisfactory for these Scotland Yards, for they then raised my reward to one thousand pounds, with men, women, and children looking for my disastrous soul in lakes, rivers, ponds, and pools. But when I, this dreaded monarch, appeared in front of them they shivered and dropped like dry leaves."

Rivaling the robbers in fantasy are the original bands, which try to present the most unusual costumes; they draw their themes from current events, or from films, or completely from imagination. Bands of wild Indians and other warriors use a standard theme to show off their varied and fantastic costumes decorated with beads, velvets,

58

mirrors, live snakes, and many other ornaments. But the most traditional and elaborate costumes are those of the historical bands, each of whose members will have spent many hours in careful research on the costume of the historical personage whom he has chosen to represent. The spectacular result is described by Daniel J. Crowley in "The Traditional Masques of Carnival":

> . . . historical masques with their large numbers and expensive costumes. Instead of playing tough, mean, dirty, drunken, or fiendish, the historical masquer plays rich and powerful for two days. He may be King Pharaoh, a Viking in a long red wig, a Sultan of Delhi, a medieval English King, a Trojan warrior in metal breastplate and greaves, Nero complete with lute train, a Knight of the Garter with authentic heraldic devices, an aristocrat in powdered wig, or any other real or fanciful personage who captures his interest.

So, for a brief moment, men become kings and princes, great warriors, fierce robbers. The political state of the island, the economic problems, the class distinctions, all seem to disappear in music and revelry. Then at twelve midnight on Shrove Tuesday, a silence falls on the island; the Christian observance of Lent begins, and ashes now mark the place where stood crowns the day before. Kings are but workmen, sailors but schoolboys, returning to the daily life of the island just as the slaves long ago returned to the fields after the wild festivities of Canboulay. But the music keeps ringing in one's ears for a long while afterward.

Centuries of Strife and Settlement

Columbus had come to the Islands seeking gold and new territories to Christianize. He found the land he sought, but at first found no gold. In the Islands he met a new people, the Indians, a people who could be added to the number of the Catholic sovereigns' converts.

At that time, John II of Portugal was interested in the route beyond Africa to India, which had been opened by the voyage of Vasco da Gama, and would grant no ships for exploration of the West. Columbus had gone to Ferdinand and Isabella, and it was under Spain's flag that he sailed.

The Genoese navigator, whom some had called mad, set sail from Spain on August 3, 1492, with his smaller ships the *Niña* and the *Pinta* and his flagship the *Santa María,* and reached the Canary Islands on September 8. He then set sail into the unknown western sea.

Spain had made a wise decision; on October 12 Columbus reached the first of the new lands, an island he named San Salvador. On this same expedition the islands of Hispaniola and Cuba were discovered. Columbus sent an elated and optimistic letter back to Spain and a second expedition came over in 1494 to settle the new land, convert the Indians, and search for gold.

But one sad voyage later, in 1498, the disillusioned colonists were in open rebellion—Columbus and his brother had unjustly hanged their

This statue of Christopher Columbus stands a few miles from Discovery Bay, Jamaica, where Columbus landed on his second voyage to the New World

leaders. The discoverer of the New World and his brother Diego were shipped back to Europe as criminals. Columbus never regained his past glories, but did make one more voyage in 1502, touching along the coast of Central America.

In the fitting out of Columbus' second voyage we see the excitement and the sense of adventure that made many men volunteer to stake their fortunes in this new area of the world as yet unexplored and unknown. The promise of El Dorado had whetted their appetites, but these first voyagers found the problem of settlement difficult and hazardous, and somewhat disillusioning. Many lost their lives through disease and Indian raids, and their morale was undermined because they could neither adjust immediately to their environment nor come upon the gold and treasures of which Marco Polo had written.

Thus, the spirits and fortune of the first settlers rose and fell as did the fortune of Christopher Columbus, who had once been honored by Ferdinand and Isabella but was later sent home in chains.

The Conquistadores—Gold and Glory

Still, settlement went on, and new viceroys and other officials were sent to the islands; but the islands did not thrive, for the mainland of America became more and more attractive to settlers. They were loath to pursue agriculture when the air was filled with rumors of vast Indian kingdoms rich in gold and silver, and so they went to Peru and Mexico, to the great kingdom of Montezuma and the glorious empire of the Inca gods. These men, called Conquistadores—the conquerors—pushed forward across the continent to discover the might of empires and the vastness of the Pacific Ocean. Dreams of splendor were once more revived, and the men would say in their hopeful dreams: "May God take me to Peru!"

The pull of the continent was too strong for the settlers of the islands, and many left for the riches of the mainland. One of the major problems of settlement is noted in a letter written from Puerto Rico in 1534:

Crazy over the news from Peru, many have departed secretly from the numerous little harbors remote from the main centers of population. Those who remain, even those with deepest roots in the island, have but a single thought, "May God take me to Peru." Night and day I watch so that no one should decamp, but I am not certain that I can restrain the people.

But other problems also beset the settlement of the Caribbean Islands. As the settlers left their land in search of gold and glory, original settlements were given little attention by the Spanish, who now began developing new settlements to protect the shipping to Spain of mainland riches from the vast conquered kingdoms. In this trade Havana became an important center for refueling and protecting the ships taking their riches to Spain. It became an outpost fortified with weapons and cargo and populated by soldiers, priests, and investors. The settlement of Cuba, Puerto Rico, and Hispaniola was at first geared to the protection of flotillas from the mainland of America.

In the vaulted interior of San Juan Cathedral lie the remains of Ponce de León, who died trying to find the Fountain of Youth. Built in 1521 for the first diocese organized in the New World, this Puerto Rican cathedral has since been enlarged and rebuilt

The Laws of Trade direct that, provided there be no special orders to the contrary, two Flotillas be sent out, one for the Firm land, the other for New Spain, and the Armada to convoy them. . . . The galleons were appointed to be out in January, that they might coast about along the Firm land, and come about mid-April to Portobello, where the Fair would be over; they might take aboard the plate and be at Havana with it, about mid-June where the New Spain Fleet would soon join them, and they might come together safer to Spain.

The words galleon, corsair, and pirate were on the tip of every tongue. Privateers struck terror into the hearts of the Spanish settlements, for privateering provided a source of adventure and vast wealth for men

El Morro, one of Puerto Rico's most fascinating points of interest, has for centuries been the island's chief defence. The Spanish fort was frequently attacked by English, French, and Dutch invaders

of many nationalities who saw in it a way of becoming wealthy and powerful and of eclipsing the Spanish ascendency.

The Spanish had been given dominion over half of the world by a Papal Bull, an edict of Pope Alexander issued in 1494:

> . . . for the sake of peace and concord, and the preservation of the relationship and love of the said King of Portugal for the said King and Queen of Castile, Aragon, etc., it being the pleasure of their Highnesses, they . . . agreed that a boundary or straight line be determined and drawn north and south, from pole to pole, on the said ocean sea, and from the Arctic to the Antarctic pole . . . at a distance of three hundred and seventy degrees west of the Cape Verde Islands. . . . And all lands, both islands and mainlands found and discovered already or to be found and discovered hereafter by the said King of Portugal on this side of the line . . . on the eastern side of said bound . . . shall belong to, and remain in the possession of, and pertain forever to the said King of Portugal and his successors. And all other lands, both islands and mainlands . . . which have been discovered and shall be discovered by the said King and Queen of Castile, Aragon, etc., and by their vessels on the western side of said bound . . . shall belong to and remain in the possession of and pertain forever to the said King and Queen of Castile, Leon, etc., and to their successors.

Even as now the world seems to be divided between the two mighty figures of Soviet Russia and the United States, with other countries threatening their control, so in the sixteenth century this control of the New World by two powers was questioned and threatened. English and French monarchs refused to accept the Pope's decision. In 1526 the French king Francis I said:

> The sun shines on me as well as on others. I should be very happy to see the clause in Adam's will which excluded me from my share when the world was being divided.

And English nobleman Sir William Cecil declared in 1562:

> The Pope had no right to partition the world, and to give and take kingdoms to whomsoever he pleased.

65

While a colonist remarked rather shortly:

> The Emperor, too liberal of what was not his own, had not the right to dispose of the oysters which live at the bottom of the sea.

Source of Wealth and Power

The Islands in the Sun were up for grabs. This was a period of privateering, pillaging, and destruction of settlements. Thus began the exploitation of this area and fast rivalries between the various strong European nations, who saw the growing importance of the Caribbean area and the power that it was possible to gain there.

François le Clerc was one of the most able of the French corsairs. With a small fleet of ten ships he pillaged almost every island settlement. In 1553 le Clerc took £120,000 of riches from Santiago de Cuba and completely ransacked the key port of Havana. John Hawkins, an Englishman, indulged in the more gentlemanly pursuit of illicit trade, while both England and Portugal closed their eyes to his private exploitation of the resources of the Spanish Empire. Hawkins exchanged cargos of slaves for hides and sugar, and in 1564 his investors made a profit of 60 per cent.

Realization was awakening that these islands, though small, were of vast importance, and the sea became a sea of warfare from which legends and myths would spring to feed the writers of adventure and fiction.

Toward the end of the sixteenth century, Richard Hakluyt wrote: ". . . And entering into the consideration of how this Phillip (of Spain) may be abased, I mean first to begin with the West Indies, as there to lay a chief foundation for his overthrow."

In other writings Hakluyt advanced three additional points: (1) the Caribbean was intrinsically important as an area open for development and conquest by the European monarchies and England; (2) the changes in fortunes in the West Indies often affected the fortunes of the European powers; and (3) that Spain, having not pushed the settlement of the islands, had no claim over them.

From sheltered anchorages such as this harbor in Grenada, English and French buccaneers harassed the Spanish treasure fleet. Sailing vessels in the harbor are still used for inter-island trade

Rewards for Settlement

Spain had barely settled the five larger islands, including Cuba. This meant that all of the many Leeward and Windward islands were unclaimed at the end of the sixteenth century. Prospective settlers were given incentive by the European powers; some could even acquire titles of nobility. Charles V, Emperor of the Hapsburg Empire, declared in 1529:

> In the deed of ownership, or separately, as they may prefer, we shall create the said founders noblemen and knights . . . so that they and their descendants and successors shall thereafter always be lords, knights, and nobles. . . .

67

However, the character of the settlers was often questionable. They included adventurers, crooks, and gamblers, and those who had failed to make a fortune in their own country. Some were modest tradesmen, lacking in perseverance. This was noted by Judge Histave of Hispaniola:

> Settlers such as those the Attorney General . . . brought over in the capacity of laborers, are of no use. They were barbers, tailors, and useless persons who soon sold the twelve cows and the bull which Your Majesty gave them for their sustenance. . . . They did not know how to work, and only peopled the hospitals and the cemeteries. There are enough settlers of this kind to spare Your Majesty the necessity of supplying ship stores for more of them.

That such people were accorded titles of nobility was indeed a great incentive to settlement. These settlements could comprise as few as 100 people and would be fully equipped:

> . . . the said settlement to consist of at least fifty married couples, twenty-five free, and twenty-five Negroes . . . a priest . . . two cows or oxen, fifty sheep, one mare, ten pigs, two colts and six hens; to establish a settlement within a year of receiving the land, and to complete it in two more years. . . .

"Free" Though Slaves

Settlement, however, was not easy for the true owners of the islands, the Indians—the "heathen" race to be Christianized. The first Spanish settlers deprived them of their lands, and even though in name they were free, the Indians were put into forced labor under the Ecomienda System. From the very first the colonists established a twofold plan for their treatment of the Indians. Those who resisted, namely the more warlike Caribs, were to be enslaved and brought under the power of the Crown by force. The meeker Indians, such as the Arawaks, were to be befriended and "civilized," though they were still made to work for the colonists. Since the steady flow of Spaniards in the pursuit of mainland wealth had created a need for laborers, the Indians would become slaves to the land and the soil.

In spite of pronouncements from Spanish magistrates urging "good"

68

treatment of the Indians, who were themselves good-tempered, the decimation of the Indian population was rapid. Despite the Spanish monarchs' ban on slavery and their liberal attitude toward the Indians, many Indians died. Some were declared "warlike," and under Isabella's decree were enslaved, though they were still referred to as "free":

> I command you . . . to compel and oblige the said Indians to deal and associate with the Christians of said Island, to work in their buildings in collecting and mining gold and other metals, and to grow food and supplies for the Christian settlers and inhabitants of said island . . . and this they are to do as the free persons they are, and not as slaves; and you are to see to it that the said Indians are well-treated, and those who are Christians better than the others.

Indians either committed suicide by direct passive resistance, died in the mines, or were killed in warfare whenever they offered active resistance. Their plight raised many controversial questions as to the nature of man and the nature of faith. But Bartolomeo de las Casas, a priest in the islands and later a Dominican monk, became the foremost moral defender of the rights of the Indians, pleading that by nature and in the sight of God all men were free. It was the great plea by las Casas, an attempt to save the Indian peoples from further destruction, that unintentionally helped to bring about the enslavement of another people: the African people. For las Casas had advised the bringing in of Negroes as substitute workers for the Indians, and since there was still an overwhelming need for labor, the institution of Negro slavery, with all its horrors, began.

Buccaneers and Trade

The seventeenth century in the Caribbean was the century of buccaneers and of settlement of many of the islands by European nations. It was a time of ascendancy and decline, of Dutch seapower and mercantile trade, the development of sugar and of the Sugar Islands, and the beginning of the conflict between the French and the Spanish. It was the century of Drake and Morgan and of the buccaneers of Tortuga and Port Royal. Perhaps it was really this century that began the tradi-

*Harbor police on duty in Bridge-
town, Barbados, still wear the
uniform of British sailors in the
time of Lord Nelson*

*These sailing ships are part of
the cargo fleet at Bridgetown.
Many private yachts also tie up
in this snug careenage*

tion of the magic and excitement of the Caribbean and that gave such motifs to numerous stories and folk songs like "Jamaica Farewell":

> Down the way where the nights are gay
> and the sun shines daily on the mountain top.
> I took a trip on a sailing ship,
> and when I reached Jamaica I made my stop.

It was the time of the great sailing ships. It was the century in which Jamaica was taken from Spain by the British. Spain had been so concerned with the acquisition of wealth from the American mainland that the conquest of the islands by France, England, and Holland was quick and not overly difficult. The first English settlement in the West Indies was undertaken by Thomas Warner. On a return trip from the South American mainland in 1622 he had noted the beauty and fertility of the island of St. Christopher (now St. Kitts). He returned to England and was granted royal patronage to settle the island (for this was how possession of the islands was gained in those days). He returned with settlers and supplies in 1624, four years after the landing of the Pilgrims at Plymouth, Massachusetts, in 1620.

This lion at Gun Hill was carved by Colonel Wilkinson of the Ninth Foot Regiment, an English platoon stationed in Barbados during the eighteenth century. The Latin inscription means "It shall rule from the rivers to the sea, and from the sea to the End of the World"

John Powell claimed Barbados for the English in 1625, and in the following decade the Dutch placed trading centers in St. Eustatius, St. Martin, Curaçao, and Saba. After Barbados the English proceeded to settle, in quick succession, many of the unclaimed islands. The settlement of Nevis took place from St. Kitts in 1628; Antigua and Montserrat followed in 1632. Attempts to settle St. Lucia during 1638 to 1671 were fiercely and successfully resisted by the Carib Indians.

The French in their turn began the settlement and eventual occupation of the islands. The privateer D'Esnambuc settled a part of St. Christopher, and later on, with the assistance of Cardinal Richelieu, the powerful statesman of the seventeenth century, helped in the organization of a company to further the French entry into the race for colonial possessions in the Caribbean. In 1634 Martinique was occupied.

The Dutch Rise to Power

The Dutch not only occupied a great number of islands but also dominated the trade in the Caribbean. Dutch mercantile power had been strengthened by its trade with the East, and now the Dutch turned

A statue of Napoleon's Empress Josephine, Martinique's most celebrated citizen, faces across the harbor to the plantation where she was born

This estate, now laid in ruins by fire, was the birthplace of Rose Josephine de la Pagène, who later became Napoleon's wife. A small museum with mementos of Josephine's life is on the grounds

their eyes toward the Caribbean. The Dutch West India Company was formed to garner some of the riches that Caribbean Islands offered: Dutch mercantile power threatened the Spanish control and later contended with growing English seapower. Dutch agricultural know-how acquired in Brazil helped to bring about the successful beginning of the sugar economy in the French islands of Guadeloupe and Martinique. The Dutch also profited by the exploits of their own buccaneers.

The Dutch seapower in the Caribbean spanned the dates 1586 to 1678, and the Dutch West India Company, after the daring capture of the Spanish Bullion fleet by Peter Hein, could give its stockholders a dividend of 50 per cent. This dramatic capture of 12,000,000 guilders

A pontoon bridge connects the two parts of Willemstad, Curaçao. When the bridge is open to let big oil tankers into the harbor, a ferry shuttles back and forth carrying pedestrians

worth of treasure showed to many adventurers and men of the sea the possibility of surprising and capturing the heavily laden Spanish fleets.

Legends Written in Blood

In those years buccaneering (as it was called then and which is more accurately named piracy) was looked upon by the nations of Europe as a means of harassing the commerce of rival or even friendly countries. Indeed, buccaneers were not considered outlaws except by the countries whose ships they had plundered. (The name "buccaneer" developed from the grid upon which they grilled the meat of wild cattle, the *boucan*. The adventurers who ate the beef came to be known as *les*

74

boucaniers, the eaters of grilled meat.—From F. R. Augier, *et al., The Making of the West Indies.*)

One of the most bloody of the buccaneers was a man called the Exterminator, Sieur de Montbars of Languedoc. He cared little about the treasure that was taken, but concentrated mainly upon the slaughter of Spaniards in battle and the torture of those taken alive. Always, he maintained, he was simply avenging the horrors of the Holy Inquisition and the killing of the native Indians, which Bartolomeo de las Casas had described. He rose to power and disappeared quickly, but his name stands with that of Morgan, the famous English buccaneer, and Levasseur, the founder of Tortuga, in the history of the "sweet trade" on the coast.

The buccaneers played an essential role in helping to establish the English and French in the Caribbean area: they provided defense for the new settlements of those nations who had not as yet invested adequately in garrisoning or built a sufficient number of forts to withstand the Spanish. The French buccaneers continued their expeditions longer than the English, for Englishman Henry Morgan was knighted after having been tried in England and sent back to Jamaica as Lieutenant Governor. He became a titled defender of the settlements against buccaneers, helping to disband the very men through whom he had achieved his fame and power. Further, Port Royal, the famed stronghold of Morgan and his men, sank to the bottom of the sea during an earthquake in 1697. Even now Port Royal may be seen beneath the waters on a clear day.

Tortuga became the point from which the French settled Saint Domingue. The French corsairs were disbanded some years later, again with the help of one of their former comrades. Many were the exploits of these daring men, many their deeds of valor, and many, too, their bloodthirsty actions.

Decline of Spanish Power

During this period, Spanish domination of the Caribbean had not only been challenged, but the right of other nations to dominate and seize territories in the Caribbean was recognized. The Treaty of Torde-sillas, which had given Spain the right to one half of the world, was no longer valid. The treaties of Ratisbon and Ryswick took its place as England and France extended their powers.

The settlement of the islands had been going on apace. The control of many companies that had been directing the trade and commerce of the various islands was soon to pass into the hands of the metropolitan governments of England, France, or Holland, and the patents and rights of possession of various parts of the colonies, which had been granted to noblemen, were in most cases withdrawn. By the end of the seventeenth century, the Caribbean Islands were effectively under the control of the metropolitan authorities.

Sugar and the Planter Class

Sugar was becoming a principal source of wealth for numerous planters in the colonies, many of whom returned to Europe to exercise power in the government, to live like lords, and to leave the administration of the plantations in the hands of lawyers, overseers, and people who had come to the New World to outdo their employers. This practice was called absentee ownership and resulted in the lack of identification of many landowners with the islands. Yet the land was being settled and a planter class was being formed. This class controlled the fortunes of the islands, and began to challenge the authority of the metropolitan administration.

Each of the metropolitan governments differed slightly in the manner in which it exercised governmental control over the islands, but all were controlled directly from abroad. The local assemblies in the English islands did possess a small measure of autonomy and could challenge the authority of their mother country, as was true of some of the local French institutions, but they were all closely supervised by government officials and administrators sent out by the appointed governors.

The hierarchy of control began with the Governor General, the man responsible to the Crown for the proper running of the government, and descended in a series of lessening powers through the various ranks of officials appointed by him and by the crown to serve under him. The absentee owners and their immediate underlings, who were fast becoming landed gentry also, formed the nucleus of the ruling class, along with other white professionals. Beneath them were the white indentured laborers, who after years of hard service and labor would eventually become small landowners. Next in rank to the indentured laborer, and far removed in condition from all, was the Negro population, which was on the increase with the growth of the slave trade.

We have said that the sea was the scene of many buccaneering adventures. It was on the sea also that the commerce of the islands took place. Rule of the sea could mean control of trade; control of trade

Old houses, such as this one in the Condado section of San Juan, have been completely remodelled inside while retaining the Spanish exterior

could bring about the increase of wealth and profits. Certain laws of navigation were passed by the French and English that gave trading monopolies to ships and merchants of their own countries and limited or attempted to completely stop the use of foreign ships. This was an essential part of the Mercantile System, which increased the wealth of each single country, at times to the detriment of the island people. This may have brought about the deadly rivalry between France and England.

Warfare and Slaves

The eighteenth century brought war in the Caribbean between France and England, and the growth of the slave trade. It was a period of wealth and abundance for the islands, but not for the slaves who made it so. It was also a time when profits were drained off to Europe. During this time the social hierarchy of master and slave was being encrusted and hardened, and local governments were being established. The wealth of the few and the poverty and suffering of the many—the luxury of the planters on the one hand and the danger of slave upris-

Vale Royal, Jamaica. The first owner of this house, built shortly after the 1692 earthquake, was one of the richest men in Kingston. In 1929 the Government of Jamaica bought it as an official residence

Captain William Bligh brought breadfruit plants from Tahiti to provide a cheap food for the slaves on West Indian plantations. This big tree grows in the Botanical Gardens on St. Vincent Island

ings on the other—formed the tense structure of life on the islands. The wars between France and England were many, and they were all related to the extraction of wealth from the Caribbean. Wars stemmed from commercial rivalries, and treaties were contracted to protect commerce and to gain new territories for trade.

The eighteenth century was a century of navies and of sea battles between fleets upon whose power and skill depended the fate of the islands, which was batted about like a soccer ball. The century stretched between war and revolution; born in warfare, it ended its battles with the first uprising of the slaves of St. Domingue.

79

France versus England

The eighteenth century saw a friendship begin between France and Spain and, as a consequence, war with England. The vast wealth of St. Domingue (later Haiti), which was by far one of the richest and most important colonies, also formed a glittering bone of contention. France supported Spain, who by this time was no longer the dominant power in the Caribbean. England had already been in constant rivalry with Spain.

The character of the conflicts may be shown by three French-English struggles. The War of Jenkins' Ear took place in 1739. On the surface this war was fought over the loss of the ear of a certain Captain Jenkins who was privateering under protection of the British crown. In truth it had its seeds in the raging jealousy that existed between the French and English. Even Jenkins' ear was enough to set the Parliament to war.

The second conflict, the Seven Years' War between France and England, had many important consequences. It began to establish the supremacy of England on the sea, and may have been one of the eventual causes of the French Revolution. John G. Coulter says of it:

> The Seven Years' War, 1756–1763, was as nearly a world war as could be managed in those days. France fought England in India, in America, on the sea and in Germany. With Austria, Russia and Saxony, she fought Frederick the Great. The winners were England and Frederick: The principal loser was France. The Seven Years' War revealed the weakness of her government and quickened the trend toward revolution.
>
> —From W. Adolphe Roberts, *The French in the West Indies*

Finally, the Battle of the Saintes in 1782, fought in Caribbean waters, brought together the two greatest fleets of the eighteenth century. Its consequences were major. Admiral Lord Rodney, whose fame as a naval commander rests on this battle, outmaneuvered his opponent, the French commander De Grasse, by very successfully using a technique of naval warfare called "breaking the line." Rodney had 36 ships and De Grasse had 35. It was customary for the two fleets fighting to form lines and sail against each other in an orderly way, shooting until the two blocks of vessels sailed through each other's lines. Then the ships reversed, and the pattern was followed again. The fleet whose resources and ships were exhausted first was the loser. Rodney "broke the line" simply by having certain ships reverse their direction and fire before they had completely passed the French fleet, thus catching the central ships of the French fleet in a crossfire. This seems a simple tactic, but it was quite uncommon then, and it won him the battle. After this battle French power was never the same in the Caribbean.

Battles fought on the Caribbean Sea were also battles for power in Europe. A battle lost meant a waning of prestige and power on the European continent; a battle won gave the victorious nation power to demand the control of many areas from which trade-goods flowed. This demonstrates that although the islands were very small they played an important role in the balance of world power at that time.

A further example of the importance of a very tiny island in the world conflict of that time was the Dutch island of St. Eustatius. Its role in the American Revolution is not often mentioned. The "Golden Rock," as it became known, acted as a supply depot, and for its complicity with the rebels suffered destruction at the hands of England. St. Eustatius is now a desolate little island in the Windwards, where only ruins stand. It is said that had this island not been the base of supply, the American Revolution might have failed.

The Barbarous Trade

Yet, important as St. Eustatius was to the American Revolution, and important as the naval battles were in the establishment of England's power, it was the slave trade, slavery and its systems, the growth of plantations and plantation economy, and the vast wealth to be derived therefrom, that were most important to the future historical, cultural, and racial development of the Caribbean area.

Negroes had been brought over by Spain in the early sixteenth century in small numbers to serve as servants to the Spanish settlers, and during the sixteenth century slave trade had been established by the Portuguese on the west coast of Africa. The rapid growth of the slave trade really began, however, around the middle of the seventeenth century.

Almost all of the European nations participated in this trade: France, England, The Netherlands, Sweden, Spain. All took part in this barter of human flesh. The cultivation of sugar needed cheap labor, and in the eighteenth century the cultivation of sugar brought prosperity to the few who owned and controlled the islands of the Caribbean Sea. The slave trade took millions (estimates range from 20 to 70 millions) of human beings from the west coast of Africa to all parts of the world. It became a source of much wealth for many merchants and mercantile companies, but for the slaves the trade meant the uprooting by force of men from their homelands, separation from their families, and their transportation to distant countries, crammed and stuffed together to suffer disease and death. Millions of slaves died in smallpox epidemics and from dysentery, fever, or being thrown to the waves at the whim of the slavers. Many slaves committed suicide by jumping overboard or simply by pining away with melancholia. The numbers of men who died in this harsh, rigorous, and immoral trade are uncountable. These uprooted men died in the Middle Passage of the sea which shaped the history of the Caribbean.

The slaves had been taken across the seas to the plantations to work the sugar mills and sugar fields, and to work as servants or domestics in the households of estate owners. They were equated with the goats, hogs, and cattle, and were thought of as so much merchandise. They were driven like beasts, working from sunup to sunset and sometimes far into the night during the crop season.

They had come, these slaves, from many parts of Africa and from many tribes. Some were Mandingo and some had come from the kingdom of Dahomey. There were Yorubas and Ibos and Coromantines. There were even the proud Ashanti. The slaves from these different

In Haiti descendants of slaves brought from Africa work, as their forebears did, clearing the land for the next crop of sugar cane
82

nations differed in temperament and suffered their enslavement in different ways. Some revolted and fled to the hills, where hills were to be found: in St. Lucia, St. Domingue, St. Vincent, and Jamaica. Others simply waited; for they knew that man's basic desire for freedom would eventually give them the organized strength to revolt.

The Seeds of Revolt

In the eighteenth century the English Caribbean Islands were called the golden diadem in England's empire and St. Domingue was the greatest source of wealth in the French empire.

In addition to sugar, the planters began adding to their wealth by serious cultivation of other crops, such as coffee and cacao. Public baths and theaters and other leisure activities flourished. Cultural societies of all kinds sprang up. Yet the planter aristocracy did not have complete control of its slaves. The institution of slavery was regulated by different laws and codes. For instance, the Code Noir in 1685 had tried to regulate to some extent the treatment of the slaves:

> Slaves who are not fed, clothed, and maintained by their masters, as we have here ordained, may report that fact to our Procurator General and put their complaints in his hands. . . . We grant to those who have been enfranchised the same rights, privileges and immunities enjoyed by people born free. . . .

But built into these laws was the assumption of the inequality of the black and white races, and the denial of freedom to slaves. Any attempt to escape from servitude was considered a criminal offense, and rigorous penalties from the whip and from mutilation were suffered by those who attempted escape. The slave laws also openly recognized and helped to perpetuate the idea of inequality between master and slave, white and black. The planters in the islands often fiercely resisted the restrictions of the laws and codes and continued to run their plantations as they saw fit. In their treatment of the slaves their only thought was to secure labor. The belief of the inferiority of the black man to the white had its birth in this system of plantation slavery. This web of complex color prejudices plagues the society of the Caribbean

Islands today. As historian Elsa Goveia puts it: "Racial inequality and subordination had become the fundamental principles of economic, political and social organization."

The eighteenth century showed the growth of large plantations, estates owned by landlords, who lived in luxury and splendor abroad, and controlled by agents, attorneys, and overseers, who were beginning to form a ruling class. A lower class consisted of poor whites who were struggling to become property owners, and freedmen—mulatto or brown-skinned—whose position was ambiguous. Freedmen were persons born of one free parent, usually the father, and one slave parent who, although born into slavery, had been set free by their free parent; or slaves who had been set free by their owners. Supporting the system were the many Negro slaves who worked on the plantations where they were exploited and cruelly treated, but they were able to persist and endured. In this century sugar was king and slavery was the stool upon which the crown rested.

An old sugar mill similar to the type used for grinding sugar cane in the eighteenth century. Many such remain, all over Barbados

Slavery on the plantation was based on rigorous discipline and very tight organization. This is how a contemporary historian describes some aspects of it:

> On plantations, the Negroes are generally divided into three classes called gangs; the first of which consists of the most healthy and robust, both of the males and of the females, whose chief business it is before crop-time to clear, hoe, and plant the ground; the second gang is composed of young boys and girls, pregnant females, and convalescents, who are chiefly employed in weeding the canes, and other light work . . . and the third gang consists of young children, attended by a careful old woman, who are employed in collecting green-meat for the pigs and sheep . . . merely to preserve them [the children] from the habits of idleness.

Work on the plantation was hard, and punishment for any omission was severe and often brutal. Many male slaves were tortured and maimed; many female slaves were prostituted. The plantation system, the slave trade, slavery, the oppression of the many by the few, led naturally to discontent among the slaves, and in many areas of the Caribbean there were slave uprisings from time to time.

The Citadelle, Cap Hatien. Built as a defence against Napoleon by Henri Christophe, this fortress designed to hold ten thousand troops was never used

The Call to Freedom

We should not underestimate the strong incentive the American Revolution and the French Revolution gave to the St. Domingue (Haitian) Revolution in 1791. All were attempts to throw off oppression by armed revolt and to seek the basic and rightful freedom of people. The slogan *"Liberté, Egalité, Fraternité"* which spurred on so many Frenchmen, the writings of Paine and Jefferson and of the Encyclopedists in France, were all perhaps interrelated and formed the spur of the Caribbean strivings for freedom. The St. Domingue Revolution, the first to bring about the independence of any island in the Caribbean, was set within the revolutionary atmosphere of the time.

The oppressed were challenging the oppressor; the enslaved were throwing off their shackles. In the history of the Caribbean this is one of the most important landmarks; for here the total domination of the white planter class over the vast mass of black servants and slaves was revoked. The Revolution of St. Domingue, in its way, may have hastened the abolition of the slave trade and the emancipation of the slaves in other areas of the Caribbean. It was the first defeat of European powers by black and mulatto natives of the Caribbean Islands.

The internal political situation of the French colony of St. Domingue in the last decade of the eighteenth century was one of conflict between the bulk of the white French settlers and the freedmen of color who were aspiring to total political participation in the government. This conflict occupied the attention of the various revolutionary assemblies in France. If the freedmen were to gain their proper privileges this would lead eventually to demands by slaves for the same privileges. Contention grew between the Assembly in France, which was the organ of government at that time, and the planters of the island of St. Domingue. The Amis de Noir, a society of humanitarians, pressured the National Assembly for the extension of liberty, equality, and fraternity to the slaves of St. Domingue.

The dissension of the white planters on the subject of the French Revolution was combined with the urgent quest of the freedmen for equal privileges. This was the background of tension and disturbance against which the black revolution exploded. On August 22, 1791, the Negro slave Boukman led a bloody revolt against the overlords of his plantation on St. Domingue.

A letter was written from the commandant at St. Marc in the early stages of the Revolution that stated:

> You have three classes of brigands to fight. First, white brigands (the patriots), who are the most to be feared. Leave them to be destroyed by the mulattoes, if you do not care to destroy them yourself. Next, with the aid of the mulattoes, you will destroy the rebel negroes. After that you will gradually restore the old laws, and by that time you will be able to suppress the troublesome element among the mulattoes themselves.

A complex outlook indeed!

But the revolution led by Boukman was successful. It expanded to all parts of the island under a series of leaders, and eventually included Dessalines and Toussaint L'Ouverture. Thousands of whites and mulattoes were slaughtered, and the last English garrison was driven out of the island in 1798. On January 28, 1801, Toussant L'Ouverture became Governor General of the newly independent "Republic of Haiti." The name Toussant L'Ouverture has become synonymous with freedom for many peoples of African descent, for it was he, a former slave, who by his astuteness and intelligence, his military skill and prowess, defied not only the might of England but also the power of Napoleon Bonaparte and the French. His name is legend, his fame and glory deserved.

In the history of Haiti, too, resound the names of the fierce and often implacable fighter Dessalines and the courageous and dramatic figure of Henri Christophe. This is the trinity that defied European military might and gave Haiti its independence.

The Decline of Sugar and the Growth of Freedom

After the independence of Haiti and the setting up of the first independent national government in the Caribbean, came the fight for abolition of the slave traffic. This struggle had its foundation in humanitarian as well as in purely economic factors. Many religious bodies and concerned men fought for the abolition of the slave trade in many European countries. The fight of these individuals involved a fight with the planters, who were the ruling class of the islands. The fight of men like Wilberforce, who challenged the power the English planters had in the legislative bodies of England, was a difficult one. But the power of many of these plantation owners and absentee landlords was already being threatened as the degree of prosperity of the Sugar Islands began to wane. At this time in Europe other powerful institutions were beginning to take shape as a result of the birth of the era of industrialization. The decline of the demand for West Indian sugar was one of

Ruins of Sans Souci Palace, Milot, Haiti. In 1812 Christophe, then King Henri I, began to build this magnificent royal residence in the European style. It was cooled by mountain streams piped under the marble floors

the factors that helped to bring about emancipation and to shape the foundations of the Caribbean economy.

Many battles were fought before the slave traffic was ended. Denmark was the first country to abolish the slave trade in 1792; the United States followed in 1807. The Swedish slave trade came to an end in 1813, the Dutch in 1814, and in 1815 Portugal prohibited slave traffic north of the equator. By 1842, the year of the Ashburton Treaty, the slave traffic carried by the European powers came to an end.

The abolition of the slave trade, which prohibited the transportation of slaves from Africa to the Caribbean, took place at different times and did not effectively end the slave traffic between Africa and the Caribbean. It meant only that those islands whose governments did not abolish slave traffic until later dates profited from this traffic. Illegal slave trade continued well into the nineteenth century in the Spanish colonies. The emancipation acts, with their subsequent apprenticeship systems, also did not effectively end slavery in the Caribbean, for the planters struggled for a long time against the enforcement of these emancipation acts.

The Emancipation Act of England read:

> Whereas divers persons are holden in slavery within divers of his Majesty's colonies, and it is just and expedient that all persons should be manumitted and set free, and that a reasonable compensation shall be made to the persons hereto entitled to the services of such slaves for the loss which they will incur by being deprived of their right to such services. . . . From and after the First day of August One thousand eight hundred and thirty-four all persons who in conformity with the laws now in force in the said colonies respectively shall on or before (Aug. 1, 1834) have been duely registered as slaves in any colony and who on (Aug. 1, 1834) . . . shall by such registries appear to be the full age of six or upwards, shall by force and virtue of this act . . . become and be apprenticed laborers.

The apprenticeship system in the English and French colonies completely satisfied neither the slave owners nor the slaves. The slave owners felt deprived of the powers they had wielded for so many years,

90

and often failed to realize that they could no longer enforce their will with impunity. The now liberated slaves, the freedmen, were still bound to the master because of economic necessity, but were anxious to enjoy a total freedom. Dr. Elsa Goveia, one of the Caribbean's leading historians, describes the situation:

> The apprenticeship was based on coercion, as slavery had been. In principle, therefore, it was the last phase of slavery rather than the first phase of freedom. It could not adequately prepare either the freed slave or his former owner for the fundamental changes which lay ahead.

Beginnings of Village Life

Freedom under the law meant the ability to choose one's form of activity, and after emancipation many slaves, by settling on plots of unoccupied land, became small landowners and formed the nucleus of villages that began to spring up all over the area. In the British West Indies these villages were often set up with the help of missionaries and missionary societies, which had greatly increased in numbers and power throughout the eighteenth and into the nineteenth centuries. Now freed farmers working their small plots of land began to cultivate cotton, cocoa, coconuts, rice, ginger, bananas, and a great variety of other crops. During this period social and educational provisions were also being sought for the betterment of living standards throughout the Caribbean area. At last the society of the Caribbean Islands was being founded and reconstituted, with men striving to improve themselves and their circumstances and to enhance their surroundings.

Yet the islands were still dependent on profits from sugar, and the fluctuation of sugar prices and tariffs dictated their poverty and prosperity. With the freedom of the Negro slaves and with the decrease in white indentured labor, the colonies turned to another part of the world for their labor. Consequently, to some of the islands, such as Trinidad, many East Indians were brought as indentured labor to work on the sugar estates. Chinese were brought in also, but they did not form as large a working group as the Indians; rather they became small

businessmen and traders. The Indian indentured laborer, however, could not hope to avert the economic doom that seemed to hang over the islands with the challenge of the new sugar markets.

The sugar economies of the small islands were being threatened by the rise of Cuba and Louisiana as sugar producers. The small islands had less land space on which to cultivate sugar than did Louisiana or Cuba, and their methods of cultivation were vastly inferior to the beginnings of mechanical production in Europe. In addition the production of beet sugar was rapidly increasing in many European countries. The methods of production were more technically and scientifically advanced than those used in the small islands in the production of cane sugar. Cuban output per factory increased from 30 tons in 1792 to 500 tons in 1870 and 1,300 tons in 1890.

There were no railways on the small islands to help in transportation, but on the larger islands many plantations had their own railways, which were joined together to form a railway network. United States capital was also being very heavily invested in some islands, such as

A Peace Corps Volunteer on a soil conservation project is about to drink from a coconut during a break with fellow workers

Cuba. It is not surprising that output per factory rose as it did. As the historian Eric Williams says: "The competition between Cuba and the British West Indies was a competition between the eighteenth and nineteenth centuries and between steam and wind."

The startling increase in beet sugar production in Europe helped even further to jeopardize the sugar industry of the smaller Caribbean Islands. For instance, in 1896 Germany was producing as much as 1,800,000 tons, while the British Caribbean was exporting only 260,211 tons. The shift in protective tariffs was a further cause of the decline in West Indian sugar prosperity:

> Known generally as the bounty system, the policy involved a substantial subsidy on exports which permitted a beet manufacturer to dump sugar on the world market, even below the cost of production, whilst he was assured of a protected domestic market. The very monopoly which had built up the Caribbean was now trained against it. —Eric Williams

Even so, all of this may have helped to bring about the increase in small peasant proprietorship and the new diversification of crop production in the Caribbean.

The nineteenth century saw the development of English colonial government based on the Crown Colony system in the British West Indies, and the fight for independence of the colonists of Puerto Rico and Cuba. There were constitutional developments, and the closer tying of Martinique and Guadeloupe and other French colonies to France. The evolution of the system of governments that prevailed in the Caribbean Islands forms an important part of the further history of those islands.

The 400 years from 1498 to 1898 were years of settlement and development of the islands, contention and rivalry among the European powers in the Caribbean; years that saw the rise and fall of empires. The Spanish-American War brought about the independence of Cuba, ended the dominion of the Spanish in the Caribbean, and gave the United States a foothold in the Caribbean Islands. Social service and

94

public health programs, and educational institutions also began to grow. The constitutional, social, and cultural progress made in these years form the basis for the present societies of all the Caribbean Islands.

The United States
in the Caribbean

For four centuries the West Indian islands were the source of many European conflicts. During that period the American colonies had won their freedom from European domination and had become a growing independent power in the Western Hemisphere. Toward the close of the nineteenth century all the West Indian islands with the exception of Haiti and the Dominican Republic were still colonial territories dominated and ruled from the outside by European nations. Even the two independent nations, Haiti and the Dominican Republic, were in such a state of chaos that at any time European pressures may have been brought to play on them.

It is not surprising, therefore, that the United States, which had been itself a colony and which was now expanding rapidly, should turn its attention to the string of little islands lying within its own strategic area. The islands had been important in the different centuries for various reasons. Now another element of their importance became the growth of United States' interest in them, an interest which took the form of economic investment by American capital and, at times, military intervention.

Here, then, began the American concern with these islands that even now preoccupies those who shape American policy. The Monroe Doctrine of 1820 brought the world to the brink of war when Ameri-

A fisherman dreams of a big catch in his dugout boat in the Virgin Islands. St. Thomas, St. John, and St. Croix were purchased from Denmark by the United States in 1917; the other islands in the group are British

97

can ships blockaded Cuba in 1962. American participation in the affairs of the Dominican Republic in the 1960's also had its beginning in the nineteenth century. Thus the fortunes of the larger Caribbean Islands in the late nineteenth and the twentieth centuries were interwoven with the economic and political policies of their larger neighbor, the United States.

An idea that has been termed "fortress America" has controlled much of American foreign policy since its war of independence. The United States wanted nothing to do with the problems of the Old World; it wanted to be free to develop its destiny and untapped resources with neither help nor hindrance from Europe. It built tariff walls to protect its industries and agriculture when necessary and to keep out foreign goods. In defense of the fortress the Monroe Doctrine was developed. Essentially it stated that the United States would regard it as an act hostile to itself if any European power intervened

At the end of George Washington Drive in Santo Domingo, Dominican Republic, there is a monument similar to the Washington Monument in the United States. From 1936 to 1961 Santo Domingo was named Ciudad Trujillo

in the affairs of any Western Hemisphere country. In order to enforce this the United States tried to insist that the seas would not be monopolized by any navy, but would be free for ships of all countries.

The United States was not nearly so strong in the nineteenth century as the boldness of the Monroe Doctrine implied. Always the threat of a European challenge to the Doctrine hung over the United States. European nations continued to promote and protect their own interests in Latin America as they chose, and the United States was forced to ignore all but the most flagrant challenges. Her own citizens and businessmen cared little about the Caribbean, for there was plenty of land in the West for restless adventurers and those who found no living in the cities. Capital found ample investment opportunities and industry had swelling market demands to satisfy at home. Americans were sure that the great ocean could still be relied upon to protect their fortress if they stayed tightly within it, but not if they ventured forth.

By the end of the century the picture had changed completely. The internal frontier had disappeared by 1890, and a booming industrial revolution had brought American businesses more capital to expend. Americans began to look for new areas in which to employ their money and energies. Europe no longer had a big advantage over the United States in either wealth or military power. Spain, one of the weakest of the European colonial powers, was also a natural enemy because her authoritarian system of government seemed wrong to democratic-minded Americans.

During the 1880's and 1890's the United States allowed a Cuban journalist and nationalist leader named José Martí to operate from New York City. He was a brilliant and persuasive writer as well as an astute politician. He organized a revolutionary movement for Cuban independence from Spain with one hand, and prepared United States public opinion to support it with the other. In 1895 his forces invaded. Martí was killed in one of the first skirmishes, but the revolution carried on without him. The revolutionaries had the sympathy of American popular opinion, but the government hesitated to intervene without provocation. Finally in 1898 the United States battleship *Maine* was sunk in Havana Harbor while paying a "courtesy visit." The government no longer needed to hesitate. United States marines landed in Puerto Rico and Cuba, and the U.S. Navy engaged and defeated the Spanish fleet.

In the four years of the Spanish-American War, Spanish domination in the Caribbean ended and American control began. There were important differences between the attitudes of the two governments, but little change in their effect on the life of the Caribbean peoples. Spain was committed to empire, authoritarian government, and mercantile economic theories, while the United States believed in self-government, democracy, and capitalism. On the one hand the Spanish felt a moral obligation to bring the blessings of civilization to underdeveloped areas, but on the other Spain did not prevent its citizens from ruthlessly exploiting these areas. The United States hoped to keep its citizens from taking advantage of the Caribbean peoples, but this did not always prove successful either.

After the Spanish-American War American opposition to intervention in the Caribbean was counteracted by two things: traditional allegiance to the Monroe Doctrine and the decision in 1903 to build the Panama Canal. Because of the canal project the Caribbean Islands assumed new military importance. They were the gateway to the Isthmus from the Atlantic Ocean. It was now of great advantage to the United States to have naval bases guarding that gateway against European enemies. The U.S. also feared that any European power which had capital invested in the Caribbean might take over if an island government seemed likely to default on its debts. Therefore the United States encouraged its businessmen to buy out foreign firms and added the Roosevelt Corollary to the Monroe Doctrine. The Roosevelt Corollary said that the United States would intervene to collect customs and see that European creditors were paid if Caribbean countries or firms fell into bankruptcy. This was thought to be the only way to keep European governments out of the Caribbean without cheating their citizens.

100

For centuries Spain dominated the sea from El Morro, a mighty fortress guarding San Juan harbor and the routes into the Caribbean

Effects of Spanish Rule

Having seen the American and the Spanish viewpoint, let us now picture briefly how the period of Spanish rule had left the various Caribbean Islands.

In Cuba those who favored separation from Spain steadily increased in the nineteenth century. Among these were both Creoles, that is, Spaniards who were born on the island, and *peninsulares,* who were born in Spain. The majority of those asking for separation from Spain were the wealthy Creoles, who were becoming imbued with an independent nationalist spirit. Some were plantation owners, some wealthy merchants, some factory and mill owners, and many were intellectuals and writers like José Martí.

101

During the nineteenth century big sugar plantations gradually squeezed out tobacco and with it the substantial middle class of small landowners who had grown it. A major portion of the population thereby became dependent on a few wealthy sugar magnates, and all of Cuba came to depend on the one crop for its economic subsistence. The rising prosperity of sugar had been disrupted by the Ten Years' War during which Cuban nationalists attempted to gain their independence. This Ten Years' War disrupted both the economic and the social life of Cuba. Struggles for independence during the last decade of the nineteenth century further continued the disruption of economic, social, and political life. It is evident, then, that before the *Maine* incident, Cuba was in a state of chronic political unrest and economic instability.

Puerto Rico had been no more than a military base for Spain in the New World. The Fort of San Juan was prominent in the landscape as its officers were in Puerto Rican society. Together with the clergy of

Porta Coeli (Gate of Heaven) Church in San Germán, Puerto Rico, possibly dates from the end of the seventeenth century and has been restored for use as a museum of religious art

Pablo Casals, the world-famous cellist, now makes Puerto Rico his home since his self-imposed exile from his native Spain

the Roman Catholic Church, they ran Puerto Rico's political and social life. The countryside had never been systematically settled, and only 21 per cent of the land was under cultivation. Coffee and sugar were the main crops, and both were grown on big plantations. Poor whites and *mestizos* provided the labor on coffee plantations, and recently freed Negroes worked the canefields. There was a small merchant class and a little light industry, but cities were sparse. The capital city had less than 35,000 people. Most of the population was white, but there was little sense of community. Many were Spanish-born and regarded themselves as Spaniards. They felt no close ties with any of the other islands. After the Spanish-American War they first regarded the United States favorably and even sought annexation. Their enthusiasm dimmed immediately, however, when the United States imposed a colonial style government.

103

Haiti and the Dominican Republic, which were filled with political turmoil during the nineteenth century, were perhaps the poorest of the islands. The Dominican Republic was harassed by a series of invasions from Haiti in the first half of the nineteenth century. Many of the Spanish feudal lords fled the country, leaving their land to lie fallow and their equipment to decay. The political life of the Dominican Republic became concentrated solely on defense and developed a pattern of brutal power politics and frequent revolutions. There was no period of peace in which to repair the economic depression and reform the social life of the country.

Haiti, the former French half of the island, had similar problems, with the added burden of overpopulation. During the nineteenth century most of the old French estates were divided up into tiny plots barely large enough for one family. Both the quantity and quality of agricultural yield gradually declined because most peasants were uneducated and unaware of scientific farming methods.

The political life of the country was torn with bickering between the small class of wealthy mulattoes, which dominated the social life of the country, and the army, which was largely black. Twenty-two presidents came into office between 1843 and 1915, but only one served out his full term. The rest were all deposed by revolutions, died in office, or were killed by their enemies. The army usually dictated the choice of the president, but most of their candidates either had no education at all or had not been trained for civilian government. Little was accomplished in the way of educational growth or modernization of the economy throughout the century.

United States Intervention

The instability of the four large independent islands at the turn of the century, plus the stated protective guidelines for United States foreign policy, combined to bring about many U.S. Marine landings in these four territories during the first thirty years of the twentieth century. As the century began, two significant actions were taken by the United States in Cuba and Puerto Rico. From 1898 to 1902 Cuba was under the control of an American military government that literally controlled all Cuban affairs. This military government was withdrawn from Cuba in 1902, but only on the condition that Cubans write the Platt Amendment into their constitution, accepting all the controls inherent in it. This meant that Cuba passed from the hands of Spain into those of the United States. Although the United States called Cuba an independent country, it reserved the right to dictate her foreign policy, to control her economy, to intervene militarily, to force her to install certain kinds of sanitation facilities, to build coaling and naval bases on her territory, and to accept all laws that the United States had made for Cuba while the army of occupation was there.

In 1900 the United States imposed on Puerto Rico a government that was directed from the United States. It was a typical colonial government structure in which the governor, administration, judiciary, and the upper house of the legislature were all appointed in Washington, D.C. These two actions were clear-cut indications of the United

La Fortaleza in San Juan, Puerto Rico, is the oldest governor's mansion under the United States' flag. It was first built as a fort in 1533

States' intention to pursue its stated foreign policy. Thus the two countries, Cuba and Puerto Rico, which had been ceded to America by Spain as a result of the Spanish-American War and which had been seeking their independence from a foreign country, were once again in the hands of a foreign government. The United States government morally sought true independence for these islands. Yet, as is too often the case, moral positions and economic and political considerations were at odds, and the latter dictated the actual course of United States' actions.

Boom and Bust in Cuba

A series of riots and political disturbances in Cuba and the resignation of the Cuban president in 1905 caused the United States once more to institute military occupation of the island in 1906. This military government lasted until 1909, by which time outward order had been restored. In that year the United States supervised a general election and then withdrew troops once again.

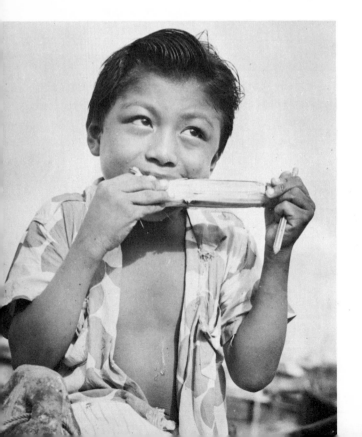

West Indian children like to chew sugar cane in place of candy, and sugar in the raw form is much better for their teeth

Perhaps because of the "multiplied buying capacity of the people," or because of the continuing poverty of the lowest social class in Cuba during a period of relative prosperity, a series of Negro revolts occurred in 1911. This was the occasion for another landing of the United States Marines. They were sent to bolster the existing authority in Cuba, and this was not considered intervention by President Wilson. The troops of the two countries battled for months and killed 3,000 Negroes before putting down the revolt.

Once again, during World War I, the United States landed troops in Cuba to support the established government and to help it ward off internal anarchy and external threats from Germany. This policy of bolstering the governments of the Caribbean Islands during World War I brought about landings in other Caribbean countries.

The sugar boom leading to what has been called the "Dance of the Millions" in 1920 resulted from many factors. The Platt Amendment had encouraged American investment in an attempt to offset European investment. During the early years of the century American capital poured into the Cuban sugar industry and helped to organize it into large combines called *centrales*. In spite of laws designed to limit American land holdings and prevent monopolies, a few American companies gained control of much of the Cuban land suitable for sugar cultivation. Large investments and efficient modern sugar plantations combined with American protective walls and the increased consumption of sugar in the United States, all gave the appearance of great economic growth. Conditions in the international scene also helped this boom. During World War I prices rose with the increased demand for sugar. The United States, fearing a sugar shortage, arranged to buy as much sugar a year as Cuba could produce. The boom in Cuban sugar brought complete dependence on a single crop which was propped up by tariff walls and a temporary world condition, the World War. When the war ended conditions changed. The 1919–1920 crop was not bought by the United States but put on the world market. Sugar prices shot up rapidly. Speculation and quick investment ended in a drastic fall in prices over the next two years. Cuba had become one large sugar farm, and food for its people had to be bought from outside.

Though sugar production continued throughout 1920–1922, the two years of bust, little money came into the hands of the workers for food and everyday needs. The Cuban government of President Zayas applied for United States government loans, but these would only be given on the condition that certain administrative and electoral reforms were introduced. An American general named Crowder, who had played a large part in the military landings, rewrote a part of the Cuban Constitution. In 1924, after riots broke out in protest against President Zayas' administration, Gerardo Machado was elected.

Although Machado's government seemed at first to promise relief from economic difficulties and political chaos, eventually it became more and more repressive. In the 1928 elections Machado was the only candidate for president on the ballot. Political opposition grew and the economy was thrown into chaos as the great depression hit the United States. Students at the University of Havana rioted, some were killed, and the University was closed. Secret organizations began to work for Machado's downfall with a campaign of terror and sabotage. Machado retaliated with even more repressive measures. Strikes were called and spread throughout the country. As in so many Caribbean Islands at the time, Cuba underwent a period of unrest, strikes, and violence. President Machado fled the country in the summer of 1933, and he was succeeded by a number of provisional presidents in rapid succession. Throughout the succession of presidents during the next six years, Fulgencio Batista, commander-in-chief of the army, asserted strong dictatorial authority.

During the disturbances, U.S. sugar mills and their employees were endangered and occasionally attacked. United States Marine intervention was threatened, and many Cuban voices rose up at the prospect of further American interference. After the United States had appealed to other Latin American countries to use diplomacy to help restore order in Cuba, negotiations began between the United States and Cuba for ending the Platt Amendment. In 1934 the Amendment was withdrawn and the protectorate over Cuba was abandoned. The political dependence was ended but an economic relationship continued. The reciprocal

Floating markets are often held where boats bring in produce from other islands. This scene is in Haiti

preferential tariffs and the maintenance of a U.S. naval base at Guantanamo were written into the 1934 Treaty of General Relations that ended the protectorate.

What took place in Cuba repeated itself in Haiti and in the Dominican Republic with only slight variations. The broad picture involves two main factors: the attitude of the United States and the internal political turmoil in the islands. There was one significant difference: Haiti and the Dominican Republic, unlike Cuba, had not received U.S. aid in gaining their independence. Yet the same pattern of American intervention appeared in these two countries.

Occupation of Haiti

In Haiti at the turn of the century there were a few years of relative peace. However, from about 1908 on, there were a series of internal political disturbances fomented by bands of mountain peasants called *cacos*, who were willing to fight for anyone who would pay them. President followed president, and between 1911 and 1915 there were six presidents, none of whom served a full year. Such political instability brought about economic chaos. Haiti gradually fell deeply into debt. By 1914 she owed France one and a half million dollars and Germany a similar sum. These two governments threatened to use force to receive payments on these debts. In addition to this, American businessmen, who controlled the National Bank and the railroad among other things, were lobbying to promote their interests. This state of affairs in the independent Republic of Haiti brought about the direct occupation of Haiti by American forces from 1915 to 1934.

This occupation was never acceptable to patriots in Haiti, conscious of its 111 years of independence. A treaty was imposed on the Haitian people and its adoption enforced by the American military. The commanding officer, Admiral Caperton, told the Haitian president and senate: "I am sure that you, gentlemen, will understand my sentiment in this matter and I am confident if the treaty fails of ratification that my Government has the intention to retain control in Haiti until the desired end is accomplished. . . ."

The American occupation brought many social benefits to the Haitian people. Roads, schools, and hospitals were built, public health and sanitation services were improved. But some of these improvements were accomplished with the aid of the *corvée,* a system in which Haitian peasants were forced to work for so many hours a week constructing roads. This system had existed during slavery, and when the Americans reinstituted it, they reminded people of the years of slavery. In 1917 the United States government had attempted to make their administrators discontinue this system of forced labor, but it still continued in some areas. These areas soon witnessed fierce uprisings, and bloody fighting

110

lasted two years in two provinces of Haiti. In these uprisings 1,500 Haitian peasants, a score or so of Haitian policemen, and one or two Marines were killed. Of course Haitians strongly resented the brutal way in which the uprisings were brought under control. Further, even though foreign debts were being paid off during the occupation, and this seemed to speak of economically stable conditions, the economic prosperity and living conditions of the average Haitian hardly increased.

The American military occupation emphasized the already existing differences between the black and the mulatto élites. Many of the former black presidents had emerged from the country's large military force, which was controlled mainly by black officers. This military force was disbanded by the American administration. Perhaps as a consequence, the four succeeding presidents who were supported by the United States were mulatto rather than black.

The period of American occupation was bitter to many Haitians for yet another reason. Many positions for which Haitians were supposed to have been trained by Americans continued to be held by Americans. Complaints of this reached Washington throughout the 1920's, so in 1930 a commission of inquiry was sent to investigate. It recommended that whether or not a certain loss of efficiency was involved, the administration of services that the United States had been providing should be put into the hands of Haitians as quickly as possible. By 1934, in accordance with treaties signed in 1931 and 1932, the gradual withdrawal of the United States from all spheres of Haitian life was completed.

Military Control of the Dominican Republic

Almost the same pattern that occurred in Haiti took place in the Dominican Republic. Here civil unrest weakened even further the economic stability of the country, which had been bolstered by loans from numerous European countries. When these European countries threatened forceful action to recover their loans, the United States intervened to prevent it and to satisfy American investors. The policy of American intervention came to be called the Roosevelt Corollary because in proposing intervention in the Dominican Republic in 1905, President Theodore Roosevelt gave this explanation:

> It has for some time been obvious that those who profit by the Monroe Doctrine must accept certain responsibilities along with the rights which it confers; and that the same statement applies to those who uphold the doctrine. It cannot be too often and too emphatically asserted that the United States has not the slightest desire for territorial aggrandizement at the expense of any of its southern neighbors, and will not treat the Monroe Doctrine as an excuse for such aggrandizement on its part. . . . The justification for the United States taking this burden and incurring this responsibility is to be found in the fact that it is incompatible with international equity for the United States to refuse to allow other powers to take the only means at their disposal of satisfying the claims of their creditors and yet to refuse, itself, to take any such steps.

Peace Corps Volunteers introduce the game of baseball in rural Dominican Republic. The Americans showed the boys how to make their bats and gloves, then provided them with a ball

A community development worker for the Peace Corps helps a Dominican farmer thatch the roof of a chicken house he is building

The murder of a dictatorial leader of the Dominican Republic in 1899 was followed by six years of civil war. During the war, payments to certain European countries were defaulted, and many of them threatened to seize customs houses and port facilities. But the United States creditors also had been hard hit by defaults on loans, and thus America seized the facilities of two ports in the north to satisfy her own investors. Fearing European countries would follow suit, the U.S. decided to take over all ports and to guarantee these countries their share of the revenues. Of the customs receipts 55 per cent were set aside for all foreign investors and 45 per cent were given to the Dominican treasury. The United States retained control of all customs until 1941. A period of economic recovery followed the takeover of customs because a stable revenue was assured. With this came a measure of political stability.

113

However, in 1914 civil war again broke out, stemming from the personal rivalry between two leading politicians, Arias and the president, Jimenéz. The United States offered to support Jimenéz against Arias, but he refused, perhaps dreading greater American control. The United States decided nevertheless to repress Arias, and troops landed and set up a U.S. military government in 1916. The United States military governor remained until 1924.

Once again, as in Haiti, the United States carried out social, educational, and public health projects, namely, roads, schools, sanitation. But, as in Haiti, the United States occupation was not popular. In 1920 the sugar crisis, which had befallen Cuba after the end of World War I, struck the Dominican Republic. Here, too, as in many islands, the economy was based on one crop, sugar. The subsequent economic loss increased the unpopularity of the American occupation and stirred much civil unrest. At this time the United States decided to withdraw, and after many delays finally did so in 1924.

General Horatio Vásquez, the new president, seemed to promise stability and financial recovery. During the first years he was popular with the people, but by the end of the 1920's his regime had grown harsh and repressive. Again, as in all Caribbean Islands, the United States depression brought great hardship to the Dominican Republic, where American investment had been encouraged by the government. United States investors had almost complete control of the Dominican sugar industry by 1920. Economic decline, brought about by the depression in 1929, led to unrest and eventually to a military coup by General Rafael Trujillo. Thus once again the rhythm of apparent stability followed by civil unrest and economic chaos had played itself out in the history of a Caribbean island.

Peaceful Government of Puerto Rico

The pattern we have seen emerge in Cuba, Haiti, and the Dominican Republic varied somewhat in Puerto Rico, although many basic similarities are apparent. Puerto Rico was not occupied by American forces but incorporated into the political structure of the United States by the

114

First Organic Act of 1900. Before American entry into Puerto Rico the sugar industry was insignificant. With the American takeover came American investment. The government of the United States had attempted to prevent the development of monopolies in Puerto Rico by limiting the size of estates owned by one person or company to 500 acres. Nevertheless, four large companies got control of half the land suitable for sugar production. The objections of Puerto Rican liberals to this powerful economic control by American companies increased their resentment over their newly imposed political status, which seemed colonial in form to them.

A series of protests came from Puerto Rican nationalists continually from 1900 on, and the United States was finally persuaded to amend the Organic Act in 1917. The United States attempted to lessen Puerto Rican resentment over their uncertain political status by giving the people a kind of citizenship and more representative institutions. Yet the amendment did not go far enough to satisfy anyone. Washington continued to appoint the three top officials and either the United States Congress or the President could veto legislation enacted by the Puerto Rican Congress.

As in Haiti and the Dominican Republic, the United States, along with its role in the economic and political life of the island, attempted to introduce social reforms and modern conveniences in Puerto Rico. Smallpox and yellow fever were wiped out, but there was little success in lowering the extremely high death rate from tuberculosis among the poor. Many miles of roads were built, but many of these were for the benefit of the large American sugar companies. Sanitation and public health measures helped to control disease, but many diseases continued to exist.

The great depression in the United States brought deep suffering to Puerto Rico. Huge United States loans—as much as $230,000,000—were granted to alleviate shortages. The sugar monopoly of the four large companies had been of dubious benefit to the Puerto Rican economy. Near the end of the 1930's Puerto Ricans began to migrate to the United States in large numbers in search of better living conditions.

Educating the Community

To truly educate a person is to teach him to move creatively within the rhythms of his land—to make him appreciate the sights, and sounds, and smells, to give him a sense of his history and culture, and to relate this history and culture to the larger world around him. To teach a person is to enable him to use every bit of his potential, to sense every part of his being, making them flow together with the rhythms that come from the land—for all lands have their rhythms. And the harmony of a man and his land, of knowledge acquired and attuned to the land around, is one of the highest achievements of education. If there is no harmony and if the education given to insure the growth of the man does not jive with but jangles against the land and the society of the land, then that education is of little use to the man or to the society.

For a long time there were few educational opportunities in the Caribbean Islands. And when education finally began to grow, it was designed not for the people of the islands, but for those who had come from Europe—the colonizers. The education was directed beyond the boundaries of the islands, indeed it did not include the island world. The élite of the Spanish-, French-, English-, and Dutch-speaking islands were educated in the metropolitan countries for the most part, and all were learning to be good Spaniards, Frenchmen, Englishmen, and Dutchmen.

The mass of the people who derived their livelihood from the land despised the land because of overtones of slavery, and they were not quick to accept any education about the land. Those who lived near

A team of high-school boys races against the clock six-hundred feet up the famous Dunn's River Falls, Jamaica, as part of an annual competition for a medical scholarship for their school

117

the sea learned the waves by instinct, but were never taught the use of the sea. It is not far wrong, then, to say that all three groups—the élite, the rural farmers, and the rural fisherfolk—were uneducated in the larger sense of the word.

So the few people who were educated were out of place and were out of harmony with the island world. Poor education of the many, unsuitable education of the few; how then could the islands become their own worlds, little portions of land with their own communities and societies, the same, yet distinct?

The Colonial Residue

In so many ways, then, the formal educational system emphasized and reinforced the divisions between and within the islands. Each metropolitan power imposed its own system on its colonies. In the former Spanish islands there was a strong Roman Catholic orientation and more emphasis on higher education than on elementary. In the British and Dutch islands there were more elementary schools but fewer provisions for higher education, with no secondary schools at all in the Dutch islands until World War II. The French-speaking islands stressed integration into the French metropolitan system, with the hope that students would think, write, and speak in French.

The subjects taught in the schools served further to divide the students from their surroundings. Martiniquans and Guadeloupeans learned about French history and geography, but nothing of their own background and history. In the English-speaking islands, the students learned about daffodils, even though there are no daffodils in the Caribbean. They did not learn about the poinsettia, hibiscus, guava, and pineapple, nor about the animals of the islands—the iguanas and agouti. They did not learn the causes of the hurricanes that sweep through their islands nor of the volcanos that have erupted from time to time. They knew all about Scottish highlands and English institutions, of princesses, knights, and barons, but little of the first settlers on their islands—the Caribs and Arawaks—nor of the slave trade. English and European history was taught to the clever students, and West Indian

118

A modern public school in Willemstad on the island of Curaçao. The statue is of Peter Stuyvesant, who was governor of New Netherlands when Manhattan was a Dutch possession

history was taught only to the "dull" ones. In Puerto Rico a full year of American history was taught and only a few weeks of Puerto Rican history.

On some of the islands the language of the schools was another dividing factor. For some time in Puerto Rico an attempt was made to teach children in the elementary schools both English and Spanish. This plan was finally dropped, and now English is taught only as a foreign language. Dutch, not Papiamento, was the language of instruction in the schools of Curaçao; and in Haiti, Guadeloupe, and Martinique, Creole was superseded by French.

119

Another division within the islands was that between a classical education (an academic education which at one time stressed the classics) and a technical or agricultural one. Until recently these two types of education were given in schools that were quite separate and distinct from one another. Social prestige was attached to the classical education; a technical or agricultural education was thought of as second best. This division extended into higher education; though attempts had been made in the British West Indies to set up other institutions of higher learning before World War II, the only two that survived were Codrington College in Barbados, which taught theology and the classics, and the Imperial College of Tropical Agriculture in Trinidad, which trained a handful of professional agriculturists. In Martinique and Guadeloupe today, the only institution beyond secondary school is a law school. The stigma attached to working with one's hands, which stemmed from the history of slavery in the islands, combined with limited availability of well-paying jobs in agriculture or industry further emphasized this division between those with white-collar jobs and the mass of the people still involved in agricultural pursuits.

The gulf between the rural and urban areas that existed in most of the islands was further emphasized in education. In the rural areas the children attended what schools there were on a seasonal basis depending on the weather, since they had to work the fields with their families. In the cities the educational facilities were greater and tended to attract ambitious children away from the land, further increasing the intellectual distance between them and their families. In the cities those who achieved success left the islands to cross the sea to other lands. Always there was this drain of the talented—from the rural areas to the cities, and from the urban areas out of the islands in search of wider horizons and greater opportunities.

Formal Education in the Past

To see how this combination of a colonial heritage and the circumstances of island life affected an individual, let us look at Eric, a young boy from one of the English-speaking islands, and trace his development as it might have occurred in the last ten years.

120

A 4-H project group in the Leeds primary school in Jamaica demonstrates calisthenics

Eric went to primary school at the age of five or six. His progress was eagerly watched by his teachers, and when they saw that he showed more ability than some of the other children he and the others who showed ability were put into special classes, there to be carefully tutored and coached for an examination they would take at the age of eleven. Between the ages of seven and eleven Eric spent seven hours a day in school, four or five extra hours having private lessons, and usually a few more hours doing homework. On weekends also he did private lessons. The discipline was strict, and Eric would have been punished if his work and lessons were carelessly prepared. At the age of eleven, he took an examination along with hundreds of other "selected" children from all over the island. At that time, in the 1950's, about twenty of all the children who got the highest marks on the exam each year could go on to the best secondary schools free. Some of the others could find places at other secondary schools that were not so good. Others would not continue at all.

From the time they entered primary school the children were divided and maneuvered according to each one's ability. Most of those who were not selected to take the examination at age eleven were, by this omission, given little choice but to attend a trade or vocational school.

But Eric was one of the few to have high marks on the exam and was allowed to enter secondary school, where he studied hard to maintain good grades, for there were A forms for the best students, B forms for those less bright, and so on down. All students were obliged to take another examination at the age of fifteen or sixteen that tested them on all the work they had had during their secondary school studies. This examination was the equivalent of the Cambridge School Certificate given to secondary school students in England. It was prepared in England and corrected there. If Eric could get what was called a Grade One in the examination, with excellent marks in most subjects, he would be placed in a special class to enable him to continue studies and attempt still another exam in a year or two—the Cambridge Higher School Exam. If he came in in the first two or three places on this exam, he would win a scholarship to study at the English university of his choice.

The educational process was somewhat similar in the French-speaking islands of Martinique and Guadeloupe. At the age of eleven or twelve the student had to choose either to continue elementary schooling for four more years, enter a *lycée* (somewhat the equivalent of a secondary school, with an initial period of four years and a final period of three years) or enter a technical school.

In the Netherlands Antilles, elementary education was provided for six to ten years. Since the development of secondary schools after the war, however, some places became open in five-year secondary schools for students who had completed six years of elementary school. The student could enter one of three courses—a commercial and language course, a scientific course, or a general education course which often led to teaching. In addition there were other schools that emphasized business preparation and home economics.

In Puerto Rico, primary and secondary education was much more widespread and followed the American pattern with much less emphasis on examinations at each stage, but there was severe overcrowding in the schools and most children attended for only half a day. Only about three fourths of those who began school continued to the sixth grade.

122

We can see, then, that in most of the islands a child at the age of eleven or twelve had to be prepared at this early stage to make decisions affecting the rest of his life, and at each stage many students were left behind.

In almost every school in the Caribbean the children wear uniforms, and sometimes monograms of their school on their ties or caps or jumpers. While the children have to be neat, there is no problem of having to "keep up" with each other in the latest styles.

Extracurricular Life

Although a student spent much time studying and thinking about his future, still the life of a student in the Caribbean was, and is, a happy one. In the long afternoons before the quick fall of the tropical night, student life is lively. In the rural areas, students walking home from school may stop to "pick" fruits or to swim in the rivers.

Generally speaking, all schools have games and sports after school, so that in the afternoon, all over the islands, in many school compounds soccer, netball, basketball, hockey, and track are enjoyed. In the British islands on many sunny afternoons one sees youngsters dressed in white shorts and white shirts contending in eager rivalry on the green cricket fields. As the red shining ball skids along the pitch and strikes the wicket, an eager young face turns around to the umpire and shouts, "How's that?" And in the Spanish-speaking islands the baseball whizzes through the air and one hears shouts of: "Ball uno!" "Es strike one!" "Es strike dos!" "Es strike three!"

There are intramural competitions as students of one school are divided into "houses" (similar to home rooms in America). Each house has its own captain, its own vice captain, and its own uniform color. The rivalry between houses is keen, and on the playing field best friends from different houses become the most competitive rivals. There are also competitions between schools.

Outside of school young people also belong to clubs. A group of friends get together and compete with other similar groups or give parties to which they invite other clubs. Dating most often exists not singly but within the group. If a young person is going to a party,

123

Cricket is still the national game in Jamaica, and international test matches are regularly played there between members of the Commonwealth

generally he or she goes in a group, knowing full well—from asking other friends—that the person of his or her choice will be there. Since most of the "dating" occurs within the group, the problem of not having a special date for a prom or other event hardly arises.

Many students belong to Scout troops which go hiking in the hills or camping by the seashore. There are some Sea Scout troops but not too many, for as yet the island peoples do not fully appreciate the sea. Sea Scouts in the islands learn to sail and swim, and row far out into the sea around the islands.

In the open air of the Caribbean, where there is no snow and it is always summer, the students, like young people everywhere, laugh and talk and dance. Yet to advance in the society, education must finally be their major preoccupation.

Plans for Educational Development

Since the end of World War II educators in the Caribbean have been trying to improve their educational systems. Many things must be taken into consideration in their plans and projects. The islands have been affected by political events, such as the independence of former British islands, the commonwealth status of Puerto Rico with the United States, the change of Martinique and Guadeloupe from colonies to *départements* of France, and the revolution in Cuba. The educators must consider ways to train youth to help the islands grow and prosper. Opportunities must be made available to encourage youth to use their talents in the islands rather than go off to other lands.

In a recent committee report on education in Trinidad and Tobago, a five-year plan for these islands included the following recommendations, which are also concerns of many of the other islands:

(1) One of the fundamental goals of the educational system should be the integration of the diverse racial and cultural elements in the community.
(2) The West Indian environment should be emphasized in the primary and secondary schools and in teacher training colleges.
(3) The teaching of West Indian history should be compulsory in all secondary schools.

The Prime Minister of these islands, in introducing the new development plan for 1964–1968 in Trinidad and Tobago, emphasized that in the development of the human resources of the islands the focus would be on three major groups—the people in the villages, the unemployed, and the young people, particularly the teen-agers.

The dilemma of the teen-agers can be dramatized by the fact that in 1963 only about one third of them were able to continue to high school.

To remedy this situation, plans are being made to expand the number of free places in secondary schools, to make the curriculum more comprehensive and include more science courses, and to put more secondary schools in the rural areas. In addition, technical and agricultural training is being expanded and library services are being extended to more of the outlying districts. Plans such as this one are under way in many of the other islands. But there are deeper problems to face.

Most of the planning for educational development in the Caribbean, as in other formerly colonial areas, is directed to the correction of certain complexes that colonization left in its wake. Deep in the hearts and minds of the people lingers the idea—from the days of slavery—that working the land as a nonprofessional is a lowly occupation. In spite of the growth of many trade unions in the islands, they feel the same measure of scorn for such skilled laborers as bricklayers, masons, and painters. Many people do not understand and cannot accept the worth of labor; they cannot admit that labor well done is as important as any intellectual pursuit, and that the white-collar workers are as dependent on the laborers as they are on him. For under the present

The Miguel Such Vocational School in Puerto Rico is one of many similar schools attended by nearly 8000 students at key centers on the island

When school books are scarce, Peace Corps Volunteers encourage students to share them. The text on the desk was the only one for an entire school in the Dominican Republic

educational system, those who go into these skilled trades are the ones who have not been able to pass the examination that would enable them to become good white-collar workers or go further into professional life.

The social gap between the professional and the tradesman or craftsman is great. Most governments in the Caribbean recognize the need for their people to understand the dignity of all types of work, and many formal government proposals have in them statements relating to vocational, technical, and rural educational developments. For until those who pursue technical, vocational, and agricultural education at the nonprofessional level feel that they are as socially accepted as bank

127

The student center at the University of Puerto Rico. College enrollment has more than doubled in the last decade at all the universities on the island

clerks and civil servants, then this type of education will continue to be regarded as inferior. It is difficult, indeed, to correct this complex of inferiority that controls so much of the thinking of Caribbean societies.

The Conquest of Illiteracy

The problem of illiteracy in the islands also adds to the general feeling of inferiority. The extent of this problem varied widely in the 1950's. In Haiti, for example, around 90 per cent of the people over ten years of age could neither read nor write, while in Barbados, only 9 per cent of those over fifteen were illiterate. In between these extremes were Jamaica (28 per cent illiterate), Trinidad-Tobago (24 per cent illiterate), Cuba (24 per cent illiterate), and the Dominican Republic (74 per cent illiterate). (The United States is considered to be 3 per cent illiterate.)

Not only does illiteracy reduce a man or woman's sense of self-respect, but it makes him open to exploitation by others. As one Puerto Rican writer says, "If the Caribbean area keeps on being a sea of illiteracy, inevitably it will be wanting freedom and justice." And Cuban hero José Martí proclaimed the following goal for his people: "To be educated in order to be free."

Cuba and Puerto Rico have dramatically decreased their illiteracy rate in the past decade. In Cuba, after Castro's assumption of power, education was emphasized as a primary tool for rebuilding the society. A "Year of Education" was proclaimed in 1961. Before this a census was taken to locate the illiterates, and nearly one million people were registered. Appeals were made to students and teachers to join in a vast force to teach these people to read and write. In April 1961 the schools were closed early so that these recruits could spread throughout the countryside. Over 271,000 "tutors" were sent out in groups of 25 to 50, with three leaders to each group. They were divided into adult volunteers (*alfabetzadores*) and student volunteers (*brigadistas*). Each volunteer was issued two uniforms, books, a hammock and blanket, and an oil lamp, since most would be in areas with no electricity. They were to either camp out or live with the peasant farmers. Most of the student volunteers were still in primary school, and one third were under fifteen years of age! For many it was their first trip into the remote rural areas of the island. By the end of the year—eight months after the first group had gone out—over 700,000 of the illiterates had been registered as literate; they had passed a simple test of reading and writing. Cuba's illiteracy rate was officially declared as 3.9 per cent of the population, whereas previously it had been over 20 per cent.

In Puerto Rico a more gradual approach has been utilized. Since 1898, when illiteracy was close to 80 per cent, it has been reduced by about 11 per cent every ten years. In 1953 a crash program was instituted with the aim of achieving a 10 per cent rate of illiteracy by 1960. While in the Cuban program the volunteers were unpaid and served for an eight-month period, the Puerto Rican teachers were paid and served on a continuous, although part-time, basis. The aim was to give adults

A youth camper, who was elecied by his fellow campers to be "Mayor for the Day" during National Volunteers Youth Week in Jamaica, presents souvenir albums of the city of Kingston to visiting youth leaders

the equivalent of a third-grade education with 180 two-hour classes. By 1959 the rate of illiteracy had dropped to 13.4 per cent.

Youth Rehabilitation

Along with other governmental attempts to reduce illiteracy, Jamaica has introduced a program aimed specifically at the young people—particularly those aged fifteen to nineteen. In 1957 almost half of this age group was out of school and had no work of any kind. Since many of them had left school at the age of twelve and had had very little to do since then, they had lost most of the literacy they had attained in their few years of school, and this made it even more difficult for them to find jobs.

In 1956 the Jamaica Youth Corps was started to help remedy this situation. Thirty boys were chosen to be the pioneers of this movement. They were sent with some leaders to a place in the hills where they helped construct their own camp by building a roadway and a kitchen and living very frugally. More boys were then taken in and a second camp was built, with the boys again doing most of the work and thus learning such trades as that of electrician, carpenter, and mason. They developed a sense of self-sufficiency by growing and cooking their own food, by learning tailoring and making their own clothes, and even by becoming barbers. Since 80 per cent of the boys who entered the camp were illiterate, there was an intensive effort to make them literate, thus increasing their sense of self-respect. In two years the number of campers had grown from 30 to 900, and plans were being made to enlarge the project since the average number of applications was around 16,000 a year.

Rural Development

In addition to the problems the islands face in combating illiteracy and developing their youth, they face the problem that most new nations face—that of developing the whole country, the agricultural and rural areas as well as the urban ones. One of the most essential goals is to give the rural areas some identity of their own in order to prevent the drain from the country and the agricultural pursuits on which most of the economy rests.

One of the countries where the division between rural and urban areas is most marked is Haiti, where around 90 per cent of the population are rural peasants farming on little plots of land. There has been an enormous gap between these rural masses and the urban ruling élite, but perhaps the American occupation of Haiti brought home to many of these intellectuals the fact that they were Haitians first and not really a little élite group of black Frenchmen. In the 1940's many of them undertook the praiseworthy task of tapping the latent cultural talents of the rural peoples and of educating them. To this end, centers were set up in rural areas. Believing that Creole was the true language of the

131

people, the élite began to study it as a language, to develop an orthography for it, and to construct a Creole grammar. They began to encourage the rural people to write folk tales in their own language. In addition, their attempts to foster the Haitian culture met with outstanding success, especially in sculpture and painting. The rural people not only began taking interest in the art of others, they also began creating their own. From that time there has been a vigorous and outstanding movement of primitive art and sculpture in Haiti. But still there persists the question of total education for that whole island still so beset by poverty.

One of the big problems in bringing the rural and urban areas closer together is that of motivating teachers to go into the remote and isolated areas of the islands. Cuba has attempted to change this situation by developing a unique type of teacher-training college. For the first year of this course the future teachers are taken to Minas del Frio, an area in the mountains of the Sierra Maestra where the first battles of the Cuban revolution were won. In this mountainous and rugged atmosphere the students have their classes under the trees, sleep in hammocks, and graduate by climbing Pico Turquino, the highest peak in Cuba. The purpose of this orientation is to harden teachers to support them in teaching in the most difficult and isolated rural areas in Cuba. Of 3,000 who began this training in 1962, only 1,950 remained at the end of the year, and 1,600 of these were women! After one year of this training, the teachers move to a more conventional school with classrooms, blackboards, and equipment for two more years of training before they are sent out to teach.

Adult Education and Community Growth

Many other exciting projects are under way in the development of the Caribbean. In addition to teacher training expansion programs like the one just mentioned, Peace Corps groups from the United States

A typical Haitian home in the mountainous region of Plaisance

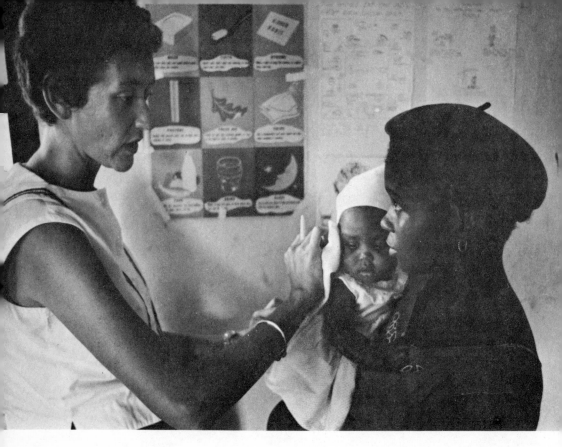

A Peace Corps Volunteer from Michigan is a nurse in a baby clinic in St. Lucia

and similar groups from Canada are participating in vocational and academic training of the young, as well as general community development. As we have seen from the *brigadista* training, every attempt is being made to increase adult education. In many areas of the Caribbean one can see adults in classrooms that children have used during the day—learning skills or trades or pursuing academic courses or courses in the creative arts. As adults pursue these courses much talent is being discovered. This talent is expressed in dance, wood carving, painting, singing. A sense of community is built up when many of these people participate in all-island competitions of dance, song, and painting. Much of the training for these events takes place in community centers.

In Jamaica the community program has become a vital part of the government social development program. In many rural areas community centers are being built and equipped with tools for the use of the people of that area. The people may learn wood carving with local woods, basket weaving in which they use local vines and lianas, and boat-building, if the area is suitable. In these centers folk singing and dancing become a part of the activities and are also developed. In some villages sports fields are being built by the people of the community with financial help from the central government. The people of each community are taking pride in these projects, and with the pride comes a growth of community spirit. They need not always look to the urban centers for entertainment and cultural guidance.

Higher Education

But what of the future of the young boy or girl who has managed to finish secondary school? As we have said, in the English-speaking islands before World War II there was no institution of higher learning except for Codrington College with its theological emphasis and the Imperial College of Tropical Agriculture. This meant that a young student would have to go abroad—usually to England, 4,000 miles away—if he wanted to be something other than a minister or an agriculturist.

What happens to a young person when he is lifted out of his environment in this way? Let us listen to what H. W. Springer, originally from Barbados and now a leader in the West Indies, has to say of his experiences. He had gone through the examination system outlined earlier and had been awarded a scholarship to Oxford.

> The business of being a West Indian assumed great importance when I went abroad. It was to England that I first went. I was not English. That much was clear, though in my youthful reading I had more often than not identified myself with English heroes of history or romance. Now it was borne in upon me strongly that I wanted a place and a people to belong to which would be recognized and respected for what they were. . . . I was painfully, though somewhat vaguely, conscious that as West Indians we still

135

had our way to make in the world. We were—indeed we still are—unsure of ourselves, still feeling our way to nationhood—still trying to discover what we are like—what makes us characteristically West Indian. . . .

I well remember how at the end of my four years at Oxford, I felt that I should like nothing better than to start all over again. . . . The thing I had come to realize was that during my time at Oxford the business of adolescence had absorbed such a lot of my time and energy that I could not look at the strange world around me with clear and steady eyes, as I should better have been able to do if I had come there after spending my adolescent years in my accustomed surroundings. In those days there was no alternative. Now there is the University College of the West Indies. Its undergraduates are fortunate in being able to complete their first degree while growing up without at the same time having to make the major effort of readjustment which is necessary upon going to live in unfamiliar surroundings among people of somewhat unfamiliar ways.

In the Spanish-speaking islands the universities, which had been established there for several centuries, still reflect the inferiority complex of the island peoples in regard to their own institutions. For a long time the University of Havana (founded in the eighteenth century) and Santo Domingo University (founded in the sixteenth century) trained people for law, medicine, and theology. The medicine, however, was hardly ever directed to tropical medicine; the law was related to European law and hardly concerned with legal problems besetting the Caribbean. To follow such professions as engineering was to take quite a radical step. It is only recently that many young Caribbean students are pursuing careers other than medicine, theology, or law.

But opportunities are now widening for the high-school graduate in the field of university education. The University of Puerto Rico, founded in 1903, has expanded and changed its emphasis since the educational reforms of the 1940's. Whereas previously it was largely attended by children from well-to-do families, it now has a student body of over 20,000 representing all levels of society; tuition is nominal and a large number of scholarships are available. Standards of the University, which

136

at one time were quite low, are becoming higher and higher, and more and more attention is being paid to education that concerns things of the Caribbean. For example, the University now has an Institute of Caribbean Studies to which many scholars from different areas of the Caribbean contribute their findings.

Another exciting beginning took place in Jamaica in 1948 with the founding of the University of the West Indies. There, in a large valley ringed by hills, about twenty students entered the first faculty to be formed—the Medical School. Each successive year the number of students was increased slightly, and by about 1950 there were about 200 students in three faculties—Medicine, Science, and Arts. There was an almost equal number of men and women. At first the students lived in long, low wooden huts that had formerly been barracks for soldiers. There, in this area called Gibraltar Hall, the tradition of a university slowly began to be built by this handful of students.

In the early days, life at the University was exciting and adventurous. The grounds were large and spacious and the number of students and faculty members was small. The camaraderie was invigorating and opportunities to pursue almost any kind of sporting activity or artistic endeavor were great. Thus one University student could be at one and

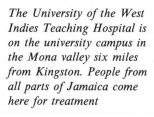

The University of the West Indies Teaching Hospital is on the university campus in the Mona valley six miles from Kingston. People from all parts of Jamaica come here for treatment

the same time a member of the soccer team, cricket team, and hockey team; take part in dramatic productions, participate in the camera club and the horse riding club and in the Guild Council for Students, and still be expected to meet the very high standards that the new university college demanded before it could become a full-fledged university. Studying, playing, and acting meant "pressing on," that is, studying through the night. In addition, nearly every night *before* going to "press on," the students would sing and dance.

During the day students wore red gowns to classes and to the dinner which was served. These gowns, rather than hindering the students, came in quite handy. They could serve as a cape when rain fell; if a speck of dust fell on a shoe it could be rubbed off better with a corner of the gown than with a handkerchief; or if a student was late to class and hadn't had time to dress fully, a gown could hide the disarray.

It was not uncommon for a student returning from the nearby city of Kingston to find his room empty of furniture and filled with grass and tree branches, in the center of which a goat or calf stood calmly chewing. At times, too, the very active research science students, having collected many frogs and toads for experiments, would not hesitate to drop a bag full of these into a girl's room. At the shrieks of the girls, the very same gallant young men would come running to their rescue.

The beginning of the University of the West Indies was a memorable time for many young men and women who before would have gone to England or Canada for education. The camaraderie, the striving on the sports field against teams from the outside, the budding friendships between people from so many different islands—all were going into the making of a new West Indian spirit. This small group of students attempting to explore the problems of tropical medicine, to look at West Indian history in a new way, to discuss methods of solving social and economic problems of the Caribbean—all were perhaps sowing the seeds for a West Indian federation and unity which at some point may take place.

Now there are additional campuses of the University of the West Indies in other islands. Barbados has started a university campus set very near the blue-green seas. The branch in Trinidad is beginning to flourish in a setting of spacious grounds facing the mountains. Plans are to have other campuses on other islands so that one campus would be responsible for certain fields of study and another would specialize in other areas. This would necessitate travel from island to island and lead to that which is so necessary—an increasing sense of unity and interdependence among the islands. Yet this beginning may be interrupted by petty, insular political approaches to nationalism. Each of the larger islands may want its own university. This would, of course, result in a duplication of services in an area where resources are still limited, but shrewd and responsible leaders may offset this possibility of disunity.

If political immaturity may divide up the University of the West Indies, political instability, which seems to affect the larger Caribbean areas, often disrupts educational growth. For example, from time to time during the last decade, the University of Havana and Santo Domingo University have been closed because of civil strife. In 1956 the universities in Cuba were closed, and remained closed for three years. After the revolution they were reopened, but with a different emphasis. The universities were tied in much more closely with economic plans for the country, and more effort was made to relate the number of students in each faculty to the manpower requirements of the future economy.

Santo Domingo University, which is said to be the oldest one in the Western Hemisphere (founded in 1538), has been split by groups representing different political factions and the standard of education has suffered by the presence of the military and by student agitation. Indeed, the University reflects the chaos that is gripping the Dominican Republic.

One hopes that the creative and expanding aspects of educational development in the Caribbean Islands will flourish, and that the political and economic instability of these independent-dependent islands may not curtail the process of education of the young and old alike. In an area made rich by diversity, it may be hoped that the need of island for island, of city for country, of young for old, may tie the islands together and give their inhabitants a sense of "island-hood."

139

Caribbean Voices

The literature of an area always captures the deepest rhythms of that area and of the people who live there. We can feel some of those rhythms if we follow the dream of boys on the island of Barbados, boys who are sometimes afraid to dream because "It ain't good!" In the autobiographical novel, *In the Castle of My Skin* by George Lamming, one of the Caribbean's most outstanding novelists, the boys do dream. They dream as they sit near the sea that moves around the islands of the Caribbean.

In the following conversation George is sitting by the seashore with his friends Trumper and Boy Blue. They are discussing a strange uneasiness they feel in their lives, though they do not then realize what it is that their island of Barbados lacks. Trumper already knows he wants to get away.

> "'Tis good to dream," said Boy Blue, "but it ain't good to dream all the time. . . . There is something real in this kind o' dreaming."
> "It ain't good," said Trumper, "'cause sometimes you get a kind o' nightmare like way we did feel now an' again when we talk 'bout the loneliness!"

Trumper attacks the complacent middle-class life to which George is being led:

> "People who teach an' work in the post office an' the bank, it don't happen to them. . . . Nothin' ever go pop, pop, pop in their heads, an' nothin' ever will."

George wishes you could do away with feeling. That is why everybody wanted to be educated. You didn't have to feel. You learned this and you learned that, and you knew a Jack for a Jack and an Ace for an

Ace. You were all right. Nothin' would ever go pop, pop, pop in your head.

As a young boy George dreams, but as a grown writer he moves into reality and accepts the responsibility of the Caribbean artists. For artists and writers in all the so-called new territories of the world, as men of learning and culture and talent, have a responsibility to explore the sensibility of their countries and to capture the mood of their area.

The Magic of the Landscape

Magic enters much of the poetry of the Caribbean area. The setting of the poetry is a group of islands, sun-blown and moon-bound, surrounded by the blue seas and by legend, where tropic luxuriance and growth of indolence, music, and pleasure are intertwined with economic instability.

The tropics offer the writer rhythm, color, odors, and tastes, the descriptions of which delight all artists whether they are Haitian, Cuban, or Jamaican. There is a feeling of mystery that floats through the islands, adding to the sense of magic. The deepest impression that poetry of the Caribbean makes is one of a magic spell.

Doubtlessly the magic comes in part from the beautiful descriptions of land and seascapes. Caribbean novelists paint landscapes of the islands in the various moods. Landscape includes giving the reader a feeling of the developments in progress on an island: the land reddened by bauxite, the land explored for oil, the land under plantation. The seascape has people fishing or boating on it. A Jamaican novelist, John Hearne, depicts a land of rivers and waters, of ravines and valleys, of mountains over which clouds—pink and orange or purple and dark—float and swirl. The sky over the island is vast, star-studded. In the following quotation from *The Faces of Love,* while painting for us the bright colors of the landscape, Hearne deftly gives us a sense of the cultivation of the land:

> From New Stamford down to the Weeping Women River it is all cattle grass, bush, or small fields of cash crops. Then, as you go across the iron bridge over the river, you see the bright, green, soft

glow of banana trees filling the broad, high valley floor, receding ten miles down to the coast, and the grey road winding among the glossy, smooth stems and disappearing round a bend in the valley. From the bridge, where the New Stamford road meets the main trunk from Queenshaven to Resurrection Heights on the coast, you can also see the tawny river as it comes out of the hills, foaming brown over the rocks, with the road covered in thick bush and clumps of trees, and in the long grass of the meadow there are tall, brown-boled coconut trees bent towards the cleft in the hills by the trade winds.

Hearne captures, too, the sea in its various moods. He paints many seascapes, and fills his novels with a sense of water in the woodlands of the country or moving around the shores of the island. Here, in *Stranger at the Gate,* he chisels out the glittering, crystallike, multifaceted shapes of the sea:

At the coast, it always seemed as if the huge, rushing tyres of the Humber had exploded a hidden mine of paint before his eyes. It was always and suddenly a bursting blue and white and green carved unforgettable, and always forgotten as it really was against the aching purity of diamond hard, clear light. Out among the black

Humpbacked zebu cattle thrive in most of the West Indies. As their white coats reflect some of the sun's heat, they can resist the hot climate better than other breeds

sharp stumps of rock, the water had a deep, vivid glow, as if it would stain cloth. And all along the deep curving bite of the shore, the coconut trees were close-packed, bent in stiff, tapering bows over the yellow-white sand and the lager beer froth of foam, with the glossy-feathered crowns touching and making a soft-lit, green layer between the white air and the blue glassy water.

The noonday heat, which so many West Indian novelists depict, brings with it lassitude or the harsh glitter from the direct overhead sun. Hearne aptly presents the noonday feeling in the country: "It was really hot now, with the sun climbing to the top of a pale, hard sky. There was the midday feeling of stillness, the slowing down and rest."

Social Themes

But literature deals with more than the landscape, it deals with people as well. In "West Indies, Ltd." the renowned Cuban poet, Nicolás Guillén, writes of the people of the islands. The opening words: "The West Indies, land of coconuts, tobacco, and rum," could easily be part of a tourist advertisement. For Guillén, though, there is no kindly welcoming sun for the tanning of rich guests; it is a sun that scorches the land where there is a low standard of living, a land peopled by:

> . . . a dark smiling people
> conservative and liberal
>
> . . . .
>
> simple and tender,
> who are the offspring of slaves and
> of that uncivil multitude
> of varied character
> who, in the name of Spain,
> ceded the Indies to Columbus with
>   courteous gesture.

Guillén points out there are in these islands many races and peoples, but still, many reactions to differences in the shades of peoples' skins reflect colonial attitudes:

> Here there are whites and blacks, and Chinese and mulattoes.
> Certainly we're dealing with cheap colors

144

for through dealings and cross-dealings
the tints have run together and there is no fixed tone.

Even though there are political parties, business firms, lawyers, and newspaper men—all of whom we associate with prosperity and democracy—yet there is much inequality and poverty. At the thought of economic exploitation and invasion of the islands by wealthy tourists, the poet becomes quite bitter. In a long tirade he lashes out.

Here are the asphalt lake,
iron mines,
coffee plantations,
port docks, ferry boats, ten cents. . . .
This is a people of "all right,"
where everything is all wrong;
this is a people of "very well,"
where no one is well.
Here are the obedient servants of Mr. Babbit.
Those who educate their sons in West Point.
Here are those who shriek, "hello, baby,"
and smoke Chesterfield and Lucky Strike.
Here are the dancers of fox-trots,
boys of the jazz band
and summer tourists of Miami and of Palm Beach.
Here are those who order bread and butter and coffee and milk.
. . . .
But here also are those who travel a sea of tears,
tragic galley slaves, tragic galley slaves.

Guillén's "Mi patria es dulce por fuéra" expresses the same song of tears and smiles, of hunger and exploitation and revolt, of a life of stagnation in a land where the sky above is beautiful and blue and the music meanders. The foreigners, people from the outside, find the island of Cuba exotic and lovely, think of it as a land of rhumba and coconut trees, of long sandy beaches and dusky mulattas. But to the natives their land is bittersweet.

My country is sweet on the outside
and very bitter inside;

My country is sweet on the outside,
With its green springtime.

. . . .

Oh, Cuba, if I should tell you
that your palm tree is made of blood,
and that your sea is made of tears;
beneath your light laughter
I who know you so very well
I see the blood and the tears.

Jamaican fishermen prepare their boats for a day's fishing at Montego Bay. In the background is a luxury liner which makes regular stops at this famous tourist resort

To the poet his land is an unhappy place where there is blood and tears underneath the easy laughter; where the person of the rural area dies before his dreams are fulfilled, where the city dweller is a beggar who, despite his dancing, goes hungry.

Three of the products of the Caribbean area are sugar, rum, and petroleum. The profits from many of these products still go in some cases to absentee landlords whom the poets accuse of bleeding the land. The Puerto Rican poet, Carlos Padilla, echoes this idea in a sonnet, "Canaveral":

> The canefield bowing in the wind
> Seems to the tourist a thing of wonder;
> But to the poet, every stalk of cane
> Is a cry which rises up to heaven.

Many of the writers of the Caribbean sing about and deal with the underprivileged, for in the islands there is a great gulf between the rich and the poor. Since these small islands depend so much on trade and financial aid from abroad, many people suffer economic frustration. Yet they dance and sing and laugh in the night, for the island peoples rebound quickly, and suffering and poverty can be forgotten for the moment.

There is poverty, toil, and suffering, yet there is music and dance. Folklore and legend spice the poetry; drums talk in the verse, urging the people to rhythmical movement. Religious observances, dancing, all of life in the Caribbean is united by music and song. In "Notre pays," the Haitian Franck Fouché advances the idea that dance and song constitute the spirit of his island.

> Ours is a country of dance and song,
> of song and dance. . . .
> It is our whole being, song and dance!
> We dance and sing
> when joy kindles the pirate flame
> at the bottom of our bronzed breasts:
> we sing and we dance
> when life tears our heart
> and hangs a tear on the brim of our eye.

147

Despite the hardships of island life, West Indian writers realize the beauty of their homeland. Claude McKay, one of the most recognized poets from the British West Indies, tells in "The Tropics in New York" of seeing a store window displaying products from home:

Bananas ripe and green, and ginger-root,
    Cocoa in pods and alligator pears,
And tangerines and mangoes and grapefruit,
    Fit for the highest prize at parish fairs,

Set in the window, bringing memories
    Of fruit-trees laden by low-singing rills,

And dewy dawns, and mystical blue skies
  In benediction over nun-like hills.

My eyes grew dim, and I could no more gaze;
  A wave of longing through my body swept,
And, hungry for the old, familiar ways,
  I turned aside and bowed my head and wept.

These are some of the themes of Antillean poetry. The sunlight of freedom that has budded the closed leaves of literary creation has given the islands a group of exciting, fresh, and industrious writers. These writers are faced with many problems, many exciting possibilities.

Until a few years ago the intellectuals on one island were unaware of the names and works of any of their fellows from other islands. Politically these islands are still isolated from one another. However a feeling of unity is growing among the artists, drawing them together. Even as the Antilles form a chain, an archipelago of islands, so, too, the literature of this area is linked together as the members of a single body.

Political Unrest and Dependency

In many islands of the Caribbean the twentieth century has been turbulent. When the foreign governments withdrew, serious political and economic problems remained to be dealt with by new and often inexperienced leaders. Let us see how the larger islands attempted to solve these problems.

Castro in Cuba

The two Cuban administrations elected in 1944 and 1948, those of San Martin and Socarras, had had popular support, but in practice they were corrupt and weak. These governments faced serious economic and social problems. Many people were out of work, and even during the harvest season unemployment figures were high. In addition, sugar was the only crop cultivated in large quantities, which made Cuba entirely dependent on other countries for such basic food staples as wheat, rice and beans. And most of the country's resources were owned by foreigners, chiefly American businessmen.

Into this situation stepped Fulgencio Batista, who seized power just before the popular elections in 1952. Batista had been running behind two other candidates in the election polls, and so prevented a probable defeat through the seizure of power. He simply entered the military headquarters at Camp Columbia, assumed command of the military and, as he had done in 1934, took over the government of Cuba. The regime that followed this takeover was marked by harsh repressive measures against any opposition, corruption in government,

A mine worker in Haiti, one of the few islands of the West Indies with coal deposits

the continuation of the unemployment problem, and an increase in illiteracy.

Batista's illegal seizure of power and his administration were threatened by many young liberals, among whom was Fidel Castro. Castro confronted Batista immediately after his takeover in a letter directed to the Urgency Court in Havana, a letter that challenged the legality and morality of the new regime:

> Logic tells me that if there exist courts in Cuba Batista should be punished, and if Batista is not punished and continues as master of the state, President, Prime Minister, senator, Major General, civil and military chief, executive power and legislative power, owner of lives and farms, then there do not exist courts, they have been suppressed. Terrible reality?
>
> If that is so, say so as soon as possible, hang up your robe, resign your post.

A school for training primary school teachers in the Escambray Mountains in Cuba. Many schools have been built by Fidel Castro since the revolution

A new Cuban factory built by the Castro regime. This plant produces domestic utensils, including 140 refrigerators a day

Not only did Castro challenge by letter, but on July 26, 1953, he and several hundred men attempted to seize the arsenal of Fort Moncada. This stronghold, just outside of Santiago, was manned by more than 1,000 soldiers. The attempt failed, and Castro's followers were slaughtered. Fidel and his brother Raul, along with other survivors, were jailed. Released from jail after two years, Castro and his followers made yet another attempt at revolution, but this effort to coordinate two armies, one sailing from Mexico and one attacking from inside Cuba, was too ambitious in its tactics and also failed.

Then, in 1956, Castro landed from Mexico with followers who had been expertly trained in guerilla warfare. Their landing in Oriente Province was not immediately successful, and so Castro took to the hills of the Sierra Maestra and began his much publicized guerilla war against Batista's regime.

His campaign transformed Cuba into a state within a state. The revolutionaries in their battle dress and their beards were capturing the imagination and affection of many Cubans. They organized schools, munitions factories, and hospitals; they broadcast propaganda over their station, the "Radio Rebelde." Men began to desert the ranks of Batista's army, where the control was harsh and often brutal, to join

153

the humanitarian rebels. In addition, Castro was quietly receiving help from other countries friendly to his cause. In 1958 the government of the United States cut off its military aid to Batista's government.

Harassed by the rebel army, by the threatened economic collapse of his country, and by the mounting opposition within Cuba, Batista fled the country in 1958, and the revolutionaries assumed control in February 1959, with Castro as Prime Minister. The bearded leaders of the revolution, dressed in their battle fatigues, captured the imagination of people throughout the world, even as they had fired the zeal of their fellow Cubans.

On the occasion of their first visit to the United States, Castro and his brother Raul, and the guerilla leader Che Guevara, were hailed as young heroes; but soon after that the friendship between the two governments began to deteriorate.

The Cuban Revolution was the first major revolution of its kind in the Caribbean since the Haitian Revolution. It was a revolution aimed at bettering the conditions of the rural areas and the mass of illiterate poor; aimed, too, at vast social and economic reforms directed by the state. This meant, of course, that the fortunes of many wealthy Cubans and many rich overseas investors were in jeopardy. Sweeping social reforms meant the taking over of many foreign concerns, often with a long-term promise of compensation, sometimes without. In order to firmly entrench itself and to decrease the possibility of opposition, the Castro government brought to trial many of Batista's followers and those who opposed the new regime, sentencing some to many years of imprisonment and executing many others. As was to be expected, the radio and other communications media in Cuba were completely directed to the explanation and establishment of the new government, and news was strictly censored.

The executions, prison sentences, and censorship seemed to some to be a radical denial of free expression, and, further, to be the action of a dictatorial government. A barrage of protest came from the United States, where idealists rejected not only the innumerable executions but also some of the practical actions and aims of the new revolutionary government. News media in the United States began its bombardment of the Cuban regime; while many who still saw the revolution as a heroic venture rose to its defense.

Yet even as Cuba rejected its economic dependence on large American investments and control, it accepted another form of dependence in the form of aid from the socialist nations of mainland China and the Soviet Union. The history of the Caribbean seems always to be bound up with that of the larger world powers. Cuba became a bone of contention between the U.S. and the U.S.S.R. Ideologies were at war, each wanting to establish and extend its own form of government to other areas of the world.

Following the confiscation of many American businesses and the introduction of Russian technicians and patterns of social reform into Cuba, President Eisenhower cut off United States sugar trade with Cuba, a trade upon which a major portion of Cuba's economy was based. The effect of this was to turn Castro further away from the American principles of government and toward those of the communist world.

In the Caribbean, *Fidelismo* became synonymous with socialist revolution and especially with agricultural reform, which so many countries in Latin America hope will take place in a peaceful fashion. The American government equated *Fidelismo* with communist expansionism in the Caribbean, and, indeed, Cuba had offered Russia a foothold on its soil. The events that followed brought the world to the brink of war, and once again, as in the preceding centuries, one of the islands of the Caribbean had produced great world tension and conflict.

In April 1961 the unsuccessful Bay of Pigs invasion took place. Many Cubans who had turned against Castro and had fled their country were trained by the U.S. Central Intelligence Agency in Florida and Guatemala and made an attempted assault on Cuba. But the spontaneous uprising of the Cuban people which the invaders had expected never occurred. They were driven out by Castro's forces and later those taken as prisoners were exchanged for badly needed medical

155

supplies. Of course the Bay of Pigs invasion had many international repercussions, and the United States was accused, both in the Organization of American States and in the United Nations, of violating the rights of an independent nation.

In the meantime, Russian missile sites were being built in Cuba. Charges and countercharges followed, with the Castro government eventually stating that the missiles were defensive weapons only, and the United States charging Russia with open aggression in the Western Hemisphere.

The United States, invoking once more the policies of the Monroe Doctrine, instituted a blockade of Cuba late in October 1962, and the world seemed on the brink of a third world war as American ships lay in the Caribbean Sea, waiting to search the Russian convoys. However, direct confrontation was avoided by Russia, who, no more than the United States, wished to enter so destructive and costly a war. The Cold War tension mounted steadily for a long while, but eventually, in 1963, it lessened and the Russian bases were dismantled.

In Cuba, food shortage had begun to increase as many workers were taken from their jobs and mobilized to meet the threat of war. The American blockade on vessels in the Atlantic, the expulsion of Cuba from the Organization of American States, and the embargo imposed on Cuban products, all served to increase the economic difficulties of the Castro Revolution. Yet the revolution has penetrated almost every aspect of Cuban life in its attempt at social and economic reform. In the face of continuous opposition by the United States, internal discontent, and sizeable migration to mainland countries, the government continues to survive. In 1965 Castro declared that all who wish to leave the country may leave peacefully. Their properties, of course, return to the state through confiscation, as the new government gains in strength.

Dictators in the Dominican Republic

Political instability seems always to have been of primary significance in the history of the Dominican Republic. Trujillo imposed his rule on the country from 1930 until his assassination in 1961. He was one of the most dictatorial and ruthless rulers in a country that had seen a long succession of dictators. Yet Trujillo did modernize parts of his country and had made the capital city of Ciudad Trujillo into a city of large boulevards, elegant administration buildings, and attractive business centers. He improved communication throughout the island and helped to foster the increased production of livestock and a limited crop diversification with the growing of rice and corn. The growth of the sugar industry also brought some measure of surface prosperity to the Dominican Republic. However, the wealth of the Trujillo family also increased with the economic growth.

The harsh methods used to silence any political opinion and the dictatorial controls exercised by Trujillo through his secret police all eventually led to his assassination in 1961. It is not surprising, therefore, that after such central and absolute control, his assassination left a great political and social vacuum, and political upheavals became a common pattern of Dominican life.

At first Trujillo's son Ramfis attempted to continue his father's control by seizing control of the military. During this period the country came to the brink of economic collapse, for its economy had already been indirectly affected by the 1957 recession in the United States, which controlled most of the capital invested in the Dominican Republic. In addition, the United States had broken diplomatic relations with Trujillo in 1960 after Trujillo's attempt to assassinate the Venezuelan president Romulo Betancourt.

Juaquin Balaguer, who had been named president by Trujillo, attempted to take office and serious disturbances followed. The National Civic Union, which was said to be communist dominated, joined with the Dominican Revolutionary Party, headed by Juan Bosch, in overthrowing Balaguer, but the two men then sparred with each other in the election.

That election was the first in thirty-nine years, and the party led by Juan Bosch triumphed. Bosch, like so many Caribbean leaders, is not only a man of politics but also a creative writer of some stature. But

157

Bosch, the intellectual and politician, faced with the tremendous task of reconstructing the Dominican Republic, seemed guided more by idealistic goals than by practical action. Like so many previous rulers of the Dominican Republic, his regime lasted only a short time—seven months, and at its collapse began the series of military coups and counter-coups that now rip apart the foundations of the country.

Perhaps the pattern of military rule, the rule of force, has become so established in Dominican political affairs that a Caribbean government run by an idealist stands little chance of success. The tragic political life of the Dominican Republic continues. Civil fighting seems to have become a pattern and stability seems to recede with every shot that is fired. Naturally the economic life of the country is suffering, social development is retarded, and the country sighs under the weight of its own disaster.

In 1964 the Organization of American States, acting on the insistence of the United States and according to the dictates of the charter of the United Nations, sent a peace-keeping force into the country. This was the first time that the OAS has taken an active role in the affairs of a Hemisphere country. Perhaps it can be interpreted as an extension of the Monroe Doctrine, wherein other states of the Western Hemisphere now attempt to keep the Hemisphere free of political and social disorder. In addition, with a socialist government now in power in Cuba, the OAS (in which the United States plays such a dominant role) feels that it is important to seek to ally the countries of the Western Hemisphere with democratic principles, and try to prevent the birth of yet another Cuba in the Caribbean Sea.

Disorder in Haiti

In 1946 there was a rebellion in Haiti against the rule of a small mulatto aristocracy which had governed with a man named Elie Lescot at its head. It was claimed that Lescot had widened the gap between the rural and urban peoples, between the mulatto and the black, and further, that he had allowed many parts of Haiti to slip into the control of United States investors.

Vendors in a street market at Les Cayes, a particularly poor part of Haiti. The Roman Catholic mission church was built by Canadian missionaries from Quebec

The government of Dumarsais Estime, which followed, attempted certain reforms at all levels: financial, agricultural, and social. It succeeded in paying off the American loan of 1922 and attempted a middle-of-the-road policy. Estime tried to proceed with cultural and social development, such as the adjustment of the minimum wage of the workers, and was able to collect a certain amount of foreign capital. In his policy he attempted to work for both the black and the mulatto interests. Yet Estime's administration was not free of a certain corruption in its exercise of power.

In 1950 he was unseated by an army coup d'etat, from which Colonel Paul Magloire emerged as the ruler of Haiti. Magloire seemed to bring together for the moment the dissident interests of the Roman Catholic

159

Church, the army, the mulatto élite, and the black middle class. Many social and educational reforms were made during his administration, and technical and commercial development took place. For a time Haiti seemed to be enjoying a period of prosperity, and Haitian culture was being examined and encouraged on many levels.

But Magloire's regime was also drawn by the romance of wealth and power into spectacular investments in cooperation with foreign interests. Too much was invested too quickly, and costly mistakes were made. For example, the Peligre Dam, erected for Haiti by United States firms, which was expected to cost fourteen million dollars to be paid from the Haitian Export-Import Bank, ended in a cost of thirty-one million dollars, with many technical facilities still to be built. Gradually dissatisfaction with the improvident administration began to spread. In 1954 the country was devastated by a hurricane, and the resulting discovery of the misappropriation of hurricane relief funds brought about the last and most immediate scandal of the ill-fated regime.

Magloire's rule came to an end in December 1956, when he fled to the United States with his family. During the next year there were six or seven provisional governments. In September of 1957 began the very controversial and dictatorial rule of François Duvalier.

As a physician Duvalier had helped to bring about the control of yaws in the Haitian countryside, and as a sociologist-historian he had done much to stimulate an interest in the indigenous Haitian culture. From having worked on the yaws campaign he had also gained valuable knowledge about the Haitian peasant class, but his primary advantage at the time lay in the bitter struggle that was taking place between three other contenders for the leadership of Haiti. In September 1957 he was elected President of Haiti.

Immediately his regime became dictatorial. He promoted new officers from the ranks to key posts, assuring himself of their loyalty by favoring them, and then used this new military control to bring the business of the country to strict obedience of his will. He elevated Voodoo priests to the position of "special assistants to the President," thereby creating religious turmoil and superstitious fear. In reply to the silence of intellectuals and professionals, he stated: "Who is not on my side is against me, and who is on my side must get involved." In 1961 he conducted an election with his name already printed on the ballot as President. Naturally he was "elected."

Duvalier was opposed at first by an organized group of secondary school teachers, and then by the National Union of Haitian Students. Both of these movements were crushed through a combination of coercion and corruption.

He toyed with United States favor by accepting aid money from that capitalist country and at the same time encouraging the bright young socialist left. While all this was taking place, the poor watched the Duvalier élite become increasingly wealthy. Eventually this financial imbalance and disorder came to a serious crisis. Population rose and external trade dropped, while at the same time the assets of the National Bank were exhausted. Laborers, professionals, and merchants began leaving the country in large numbers. As the crisis increased, the government became more and more unreasonable in dealing with it. The opposition to Duvalier was also splintered into factions, and most of these small factions found themselves bloodily crushed.

This situation of disorder has continued in differing degrees of intensity until the present day. The violently nationalistic Duvalier seems to confine his activities to his own country, and none of the powerful interests in the Caribbean have seriously attempted to interfere with his personal dictatorship. In spite of external condemnation of his regime and persistent opposition to his rule by many Haitians in exile, Duvalier has ruled Haiti for more than nine years now. One wonders how this shrewd political leader—"Papa Doc" as he is now called by friend and foe alike—is able to maintain his power.

The Commonwealth of Puerto Rico

In Puerto Rico the party system functions in principle; but in fact, for the past eighteen years the country has been controlled by one party, the Popular Democratic Party, headed by the astute statesman Muñoz Marín. Until 1965, when his political lieutenant Roberto Sanchez-

A modern ranch-style house in a high-income, residential area of Puerto Rico

Vilella was elected to the governorship, Marín was the governor of Puerto Rico, and still wields an amazing degree of political power.

During the 1940's there were many constitutional discussions in Washington relating to the status of Puerto Rico, and in 1947 a measure of autonomy was given the island when the governor became an elected official and was no longer appointed from Washington. In this election Muñoz Marín was triumphant. In 1950 a new constitution was created and adopted by a local constitutional convention, and in 1952 Puerto Rico became a commonwealth.

Muñoz Marín was not only governor of the island, but also the head of the party in power. Since the party held the majority of seats in both houses, it meant that Marín, as head of the party, in effect had control of both the legislative and executive branches of the government. Consequently, any opposition to bills presented in the two houses could easily be crushed since both houses were controlled by the party, and within this democratic framework dissension was limited. There were voices raised in opposition to government policies, but the opposition was directed more toward the essential problem of the status of Puerto Rico under the government of the United States than toward debate of internal affairs. That the United States financial assistance was helping to raise standards of living was evident. Yet many Puerto Ricans saw this help as another form of exploitation and reasoned that Puerto Rico was in fact a colony of the United States.

Low-income blocks of apartments in San Juan, Puerto Rico

The relationship between Puerto Rico and the United States can be equated with that of a parent and child. Should a young person be given a large allowance by his rich parent to help him along as he grows up, making him dependent but also quickening his growth, or should a young person strive to find his own way by his own efforts, even when such striving means much hardship? This situation is the most essential dilemma facing the Puerto Rican people. Should Puerto Rico be a state within the United States, enjoying all the privileges this would bring about? Should it have a commonwealth status, which gives it a certain amount of autonomy and control of its own affairs, as well as a certain dependence on the United States? Or should it be an independent and separate country having complete control over all of its affairs?

Its commonwealth status means that Puerto Rico is self-governing in all local matters, but that its foreign relationships and position in the international world are controlled by the United States. Because of this status Puerto Rico has no seat in the United Nations as do Cuba, Haiti, Jamaica, Trinidad and Tobago. However, Puerto Rico pays no federal taxes, and all duties collected on Puerto Rican goods by United States customs go into the Puerto Rican treasury. In addition, many programs of internal development are completely financed by the United States. Puerto Rico, however, has no vote in Congress because it pays no taxes to support the United States Government.

The commonwealth status of Puerto Rico seems acceptable to the Popular Democratic Party, but the separatists or *Independentistas,* those who want separation from the United States, think Puerto Rico should be free of the United States and should attempt to have complete control of its own affairs. These *Independentistas* include many university students and liberals. The importance for some of these liberals of the political relationship between Puerto Rico and the United States has been dramatized on several occasions. In 1950, for example, a Puerto Rican patriot attempted to assassinate the President of the United States, Harry Truman. The question of Puerto Rico's status is perhaps the principal factor giving rise to protest marches and demonstrations and a measure of political unrest within the island itself.

The future of Puerto Rico depends to a large extent on whether the *Independentistas* and those seeking complete national autonomy will attempt to forcefully change the pattern of political government, or whether the party which has been in control for so long, and which has the complete support of the United States, can continue to be elected and to show the benefits that come from an ambiguous political position.

Self-Government in the British West Indies

For more than 300 years England controlled the destiny of the English-speaking Caribbean Islands. By settlement, by purchase, and by capture, England had seized and governed and colonized. Even though its power was often challenged, especially by the island governments, England held complete control of the islands until 1944, when Jamaica became the first to gain a somewhat greater measure of control over its own affairs, a major step toward its independence.

Two major concerns have dominated the political and constitutional life of the British West Indies since 1940: first, the movement in many islands toward self-government and eventual independence, and second, the attempt to unify the British West Indian islands into a federation.

Control of their destiny from outside, and the inability to shake off imperial domination, was the lot of the Caribbean Islands. The islands were colonies ruled under a system of Crown Colony government, and even though Barbados was never, constitutionally speaking, a Crown Colony, yet its relation to England was virtually that of a dependent colony to its mother country. In the case of all the other islands, to be a Crown Colony meant that the affairs of the legislative and executive councils were in the hands of administrators sent out from England.

A typical Crown Colony government would be headed by the representative of the Crown of England, the governor or administrator, who wielded an almost absolute power and had the last say in local as well as external matters. In legislation, finance, affairs of state, control of the military and police forces, and the control of commerce, indeed in the control of all the affairs of the island, decision rested in the hands of

165

persons sent from England as the Colonial Secretary, Attorney General, Trade Commissioner, and so forth.

At first Crown Colony governments were governments in which the voice of the people was usually muffled. Even when these voices were raised they were virtually powerless to advocate the wishes of the people. That which is called the Colonial System was built upon the principle that the peoples of the territory governed by the "mother country" should be carefully tutored and helped along until such time as they could direct their own affairs.

For many years far-sighted leaders in the colonies themselves requested that the peoples of the various islands govern themselves and be masters of their own affairs. In the nineteenth century the planter class had made many requests for increased independence in the regulation of their affairs, although such requests did not take into consid-

Princess Margaret greets a welcoming dignitary as she arrives in Trinidad on a state visit

The Savannah in Port-of-Spain, Trinidad, is a park for horse racing, cricket, and soccer as well as a recreation ground

eration the total good of the community but were more concerned with bettering the planter class. However, other leaders, with the interests of the West Indies at heart, were also demanding more control over their own affairs.

In 1917 one of the English Caribbean's oldest and most energetic statesmen, T. M. Marryshow, requested:

> . . . that this West Indies must be a new West Indies in the new world that shall dawn as a result of the war, and that she is convinced such a new West Indies is dependent on a more dignified and respectable form of government which alone can justify our elevation to the inter-imperial citizenship of empire.

This is but one of the many statements beginning to be made by several leaders. The voices of Arthur Cipriani and Uriah Butler were raised in Trinidad, that of Grantley Adams in Barbados, and those of Norman Manley and Alexander Bustamante in Jamaica. These leaders

167

were of all classes and of all types. Some were self-educated and some were scholars from Oxford or Cambridge; some were trade unionists and some were school teachers. These were, and some still are, colorful leaders who, imbued with the sense of national pride, worked zealously to bring about self-government in the English-speaking Caribbean. It is true that with time some of these leaders may have lost a sense of the total vision of nationhood, yet their fight for self-government must always be remembered. They were forerunners of younger men now directing the destinies of the Caribbean.

Jamaica was the first island in the British West Indies to gain total independence—in 1962. Trinidad also had progressed from increased local representation in the ruling executive councils in 1959 to total independence in 1962; and Barbados became an independent state in 1966.

The other islands also became increasingly self-governing. In the Windward and Leeward islands, constitutional reform took place during the fifties, leading to the establishment of ministerial governments. For many years there had been a governor of the Leeward group of islands (Antigua, St. Kitts, Nevis-Anguilla, Montserrat), with a headquarters in Antigua, and a government in the Windward islands (Grenada, St. Lucia, St. Vincent, and Dominica) with a headquarters in Grenada. The Windward and Leeward islands also have now moved to the point of independence. For instance, the Constitution of Antigua, which is similar to that of many of these islands, is constructed to create:

> A parliament in Antigua comprising her Majesty the Queen, a Senate, and a House of Representatives. There shall be a Governor, who shall be the Queen's Representative . . . the executive shall comprise a cabinet consisting of a Premier and other Ministers. The Premier shall be approved by the Governor on the advice of the Parliament. The Governor shall be bound to accept the advice of the Cabinet in the exercise of his functions.

For some time the island of Grenada had hoped to join the independent unit of Trinidad and Tobago. Many of the other islands are so small that independence as single units would be almost meaningless unless they were to bind together and form a free and united federation. The future relationship of the self-governing but nonindependent islands with the British government is ambiguous. It is possible that the British government, busy with its own affairs, may be only too willing to grant independence to these little islands. But now they have been offered a political relationship as Home-rule States associated with Britain, and are able to request total independence whenever they choose. Under this new political arrangement, the islands would control their own internal affairs, although Britain would continue to discharge responsibility for their external affairs and defense. The British government would have a Queen's representative to conduct its relationships in each island. The islands would continue to be eligible for British aid, following much the same pattern as other countries of the Commonwealth.

In all of these islands, where for so long universal adult suffrage did not prevail and where for so long allegiance was to England, attitudes fostered by colonialism still remain. Too often the peoples of the English-speaking Caribbean continue to adopt English institutions that ill-suit their own communities, and too often a person's social position stems from the lightness of his skin.

All of the islands have inherited the constitutional parliamentary system of government of the United Kingdom and still adhere to the party system, with its ministerial setup. Under this system of government the ministers of trade, development, and so forth are drawn from the ranks of the party winning the election; the head of the party forms the government and becomes the Prime Minister, and the losing parties form opposition blocks in the legislative chambers. Should these opposition parties succeed in forcing a vote of no-confidence in the party in power, general elections would then be called for.

The question is often raised as to whether this type of government, inherited from the United Kingdom, is the one best suited to direct the affairs of these small islands. At any rate, within the past decade the peoples of the English-speaking Caribbean islands have become quite politically conscious, and are increasingly aware of political issues.

One of the most amazing and dynamic growths in political interest took place in Trinidad in the 1950's when its new Prime Minister, Eric Williams, created what is now known as the University of Woodford Square. Night after night, even before the campaign and the formation of his party, this political leader addressed thousands of citizens who crammed into a tiny park to hear of the political and constitutional disputes, the trade and economic balance, the relationship of freedom to independence, and many more important issues. For several years even the smallest child knew the name of this leader, could tell you the title of his next lecture, and may even have been able to tell you something about the lecture itself. It was truly a time of vital political ferment within the island.

The coming of independence to some of the British West Indian islands, and the prospective independence of others, has placed a heavy responsibility for wise government on the shoulders of many political leaders and parties, but has also brought with it the excitement of attempting to rule one's own destiny.

Dreams of Federation

During the fifties the peoples of the British West Indian islands were caught up in the question of the federation of their islands. At this time the West Indian Federation was formed, but was soon disbanded. It was perhaps the shortest federation of states in the history of the modern world, and with its dissolution went the hopes of many young West Indians. Many of these young people feel that in federation they can achieve a feeling of size and space they do not have within each small island. The people of the islands are a traveling people, and even more than the possible political benefits brought about by federation, the desire to visit the other islands of the federation and the chance to travel more easily among them would give the people a breadth of freedom through movement.

In addition, many young West Indians who have traveled far abroad to England, the United States, Europe, or Africa are extremely conscious of the smallness of the island units and the great need for a federated

170

group of islands. They have met together on sports' fields, during inter-island matches in cricket, soccer, tennis, table-tennis, and water polo, and in study at the University of the West Indies. Abroad they have found that wherever they go they are no longer a person from Barbados or Grenada or Trinidad, but are West Indians.

Yet despite the many ties and bonds between the islands, there continues to exist an amazing insularity that has consistently worked against these ties and brought about jealous rivalries. Consequently, communication and travel between the islands was for a long time relatively small.

Whatever the ties that united or the lack of communication that divided these islands, the idea of federation has been fostered since the

Passengers crowd the decks of a coastal boat. There is a need for more traffic between the islands

early part of the century. Many attempts to federate the islands have been made, but all have failed.

In 1922 Major E. P. Wood, in the course of an investigation of disturbance in Trinidad, reported that it was "both inopportune and impracticable" to allow the islands to federate at that time. Opinions changed, however, as the islands seemed to grow more stable in their government.

In 1947 a conference on federation was held at Montego Bay in Jamaica, and a Standing Closer Association Committee was formed to study the possibility of federation and to draft a constitution. At the London Conferences in 1953 and 1956, it was decided that the federation would consist of two bodies: a senate of nineteen members, with

An aerial view of Curaçao shows the oil refineries which are the island's main source of income

one or two nominated from each island by the respective governor-generals, and a house of representatives, with its membership allocated on the basis of population. The system was to follow closely the pattern of that in the United Kingdom, but the Queen would retain certain overriding legislative powers in respect to defense, maintenance of public and financial order, and foreign relations. Thus, in 1960, the Federation of the Caribbean Islands was formed. However, in 1962 Jamaica withdrew from the Federation to seek independence, and Trinidad and Tobago followed. The remaining islands, deprived of the participation of these largest territories, subsequently abandoned the idea of West Indian federation.

With the failure of the larger federation and the independence of Jamaica and Trinidad and Tobago, attempts were made to form a Southern Caribbean Federation merging Barbados and the Leeward and Windward islands. These attempts were unsuccessful, and with the recent independence of Barbados now have little chance of succeeding.

At present a federation of the islands exists only in the minds and hopes of young men as a desirable possibility, indeed a necessity. Perhaps after the excitement of individual independence lessens the isolating nationalism of the various islands, their federation will take place.

The French and Dutch West Indies

The French Caribbean islands of Martinique and Guadeloupe, and the Dutch West Indian islands of Curaçao and Aruba, and other small Dutch territories in the Caribbean, are still constitutionally tied to their mother countries.

Ever since the French Revolution, Martinique and Guadeloupe have had representation within the French National Assembly, sending deputies to that assembly and yet still retaining the status of a colony of France. In 1946, however, by a new constitutional arrangement, the islands lost their colonial status and became *départements* of France. The governors of the islands were replaced by prefects, and Martinique and Guadeloupe now come directly under the social, economic, and political administration of France. In all respects they are a part of France, which happens not to be on the mainland of France but over-

Schooners from nearby islands bring fish, fruit, vegetables, and handicrafts from nearby islands for the inhabitants of Curaçao. The turtle on its back is destined for a soup factory

seas. The people of the islands vote in the French elections and send representatives to the French assembly; but this relationship to France is not welcomed by liberal thinkers in these islands or by the left-wing communist party, which plays a large part in the local assemblies.

For instance, this election manifesto from a political party in Martinique states a forceful opposition to the departmentalization of the island:

174

> . . . a quick glance at its economic, social, political and cultural
> makeup shows that our country is a very different country from
> France; ours is a colonial country, a country ruled by imperial-
> ism. . . . Everywhere throughout the world today, colonial peoples
> are fighting for their independence. . . . The Martiniquais must take
> a much greater part in the management of their own affairs.

This ambiguous political relationship seems to have awakened the nationalist sentiments of the Martiniquais and the people of Guadeloupe; and may lead them very soon to reject their status as *départements* of France and seek total independence.

The relationship between the Dutch West Indies and Holland is similar to that between the French West Indies and France; but perhaps their relationship resembles more that between Puerto Rico and the United States. The difference is that, while Puerto Rico has never been given the opportunity to send representatives to the United States Congress, Curaçao and Aruba were offered such representation in the Hague but they refused this offer. They have an autonomous status, but the Netherlands retains control of foreign and defense policies. The Queen of the Netherlands is head of the government of the Netherlands Antilles; and she appoints a governor who administers the islands along with a council of ministers appointed by him. The ministers must receive recommendations from the Legislative Council, and they are responsible to it for their policy. The Council consists of twenty-two members elected for periods of four years on a system of universal suffrage.

All the West Indian islands, even the independent republics, still seem politically tied to and dominated by foreign powers: England, France, the Netherlands, the Union of Soviet Socialist Republics, and the United States. One wonders if these Caribbean islands will ever achieve the identity of a strong codependence or a strong and meaningful individual independence.

Economic Life and Prospects

And the trees run down to the sea, ride the hump of hills, climb up mountains, plunge into valleys, march in groves over the flat lands. The coconut tree, arched against the horizon, dances in the sea wind; the huge green fruits crest the tree and lose themselves amid the palm fronds. Columbus delighted in the "delicious freshness" of their shade; and in the abundant flowers and fruits of the West Indies he found a "beauty and conveniency" which "far surpass all the rest of the world."

Indeed, the islands are rich in their fruits: the guavas and tamarinds, star and custard apples, sapodillas and sugar apples, and soursops—or guanabanas, as they are called in the Spanish islands. Papayas hang heavy from the branches of trees, light green when ripening, golden-yellow and sweet when ripe. And pineapples, sweet also under their rough prickly skin, thrust their green spears up from the ground.

The Spaniards brought with them the bananas and citrus fruits—oranges, tangerines, grapefruit, lemons, limes—which flourish in the good soil and sunny climate of the Caribbean. Later the ackee tree came along with the slaves from West Africa, and today its bright yellow fruit is eaten along with salt fish as the national dish of Jamaica. The mango, too, came with the slave trade and spread over the islands in all its many varieties: Bombay, St. Julian, "Doudouce," Turpentine, Calabash mangoes. In the mango season, the sweet rich fruit is picked by the women to be sold or "t'iefed" by school children for a quick feast. The breadfruit was brought to the Caribbean from the Polynesian islands by the Europeans, who hoped to use the big starchy fruit as an

Linstead Market, where life goes on much in the same way as it has for centuries, is in sharp contrast to the modern town of Linstead with its up-to-date factories

177

inexpensive food for their slaves. Although the plant thrived and is much used today, the slaves for a long time preferred their own crops: plantains and the ground provisions, cassava, yams, tanias, edoes, and dasheen, which still form the basic diet for many of the people of the West Indies.

In this luxuriant climate also flourished the crops that would form the basis of the Caribbean economy. The Europeans found tobacco when they arrived; and for some time this novelty was the chief West Indian export to the European markets. The colonial settlers also cultivated for export cacao, coffee, cotton, and such specialties as indigo, arrowroot, and spices: ginger, nutmeg, mace, pimento. But the great development of the export economy came with the introduction of sugar cane, which grew easily and spread through the Caribbean.

"Feast and Famine" Side by Side

All West Indians revel in the fine climate and natural beauty of their islands, but they do not all share equally in the economic riches. Many people exist barely above a subsistence level, with ground provisions as the main food in their diets. But there are some who live in plenty; and the contrast in living standards between the impoverished and the wealthy is everywhere apparent.

An agricultural expert of St. Vincent holds a stemless pod from one of the many cocoa trees which grow there free from diseases that attack these trees. The greasy cocoa seeds inside the pod are removed, washed, and roasted to form the basis for chocolate

The black seed of the nutmeg tree is covered with a waxy substance called mace; both are valued spices. Nutmeg trees reach a height of ninety feet in Grenada and Dominica which supply 80% of the world's nutmeg and mace

If, for example, we swing along the north coast road in Jamaica, traveling west from the tourist town of Montego Bay, we see first the wealthy suburbs, with their big new houses set back from the road, surrounded by landscaped gardens and fruit trees, often running down to private beaches where luxury yachts are anchored. Everywhere here the landscape is beautiful to behold.

But in this same landscape, a little further on, a few small wooden shacks stand hugging the road, the nucleus of a fishing village of a few hundred souls. Their small wooden boats lie close to the shore, waiting for the nightly fishing expeditions. The life of the fishermen is hard, for as yet they have not been taught new fishing techniques, and it is only their skill and endurance that enables them to make a moderate catch.

Most of this catch is sold, and the money used to buy basic necessities from a small country store, which contains just about everything that the community uses for its meager living. Here, too, men gather to play jacks or dominoes and women meet to share the local gossip. These are minor pleasures of a poor community. Perhaps now with the projected community development, all these villages will be transformed. The wealthy suburbs need no such transformation, for huge golf links, private swimming pools, and tennis courts provide pleasurable occupation for leisure hours.

If we turn to the interior of the island, driving along the winding, twisting roads, we are struck by a similar contrast between the huge plantations which grow crops for export and the small plots of land where people grow ground provisions and raise some poultry—just enough to feed themselves with a little left over to sell in the local market. If we were on the road early in the morning, we would hear the crowing of roosters and the flapping of hens' wings from the small yards, and we would see the village folk driving their fresh produce to the market on donkey carts or carrying it in baskets balanced on their heads. West Indian folk songs tell of the fortunes of the markets, including "Linstead Market," where the lady's luck was not good:

> Carry me ackee go a Linstead Market,
> Not a quatty wut sell.
> Carry me ackee go a Linstead Market,
> Not a quatty wut sell.
>
> Oh, Lawd! Not a mite not a bite,
> Wat a Satiday night!
> Lawd! Not a mite not a bite,
> Wat a Satiday night.

The market is a colorful place, with the many fruits spread out for display. One can buy fresh fish, meat, eggs, and live fowls. Sometimes there are earthenware goblets and handmade straw goods for sale. The bargaining is lively, with noise and bustle, quick quarrels and friendly laughter.

180

A few such markets are found in the cities, but most of them are in the country districts. They are quite different from the modern super-markets in and around the cities. In the cities also is the contrast between new and old, rich and poor. Donkey carts jostle against the latest models of American and European automobiles. In front of department stores and modern restaurants, women peddle food and drinks and men sell fresh coconuts, cutting them open with a machete so that their customers can drink the cool, refreshing liquid straight from the fruit.

Population and Unemployment

Going out from the heart of the city, we are struck by the contrast between lovely suburbs with tree-lined streets and comfortable houses on the one hand, and unsightly slums with filthy lanes and squalid shacks on the other. Often many of the people in these slums are unemployed, and among them there are feelings of unrest and anger at their lot.

This residential area of Belleville, Barbados, is renowned for its avenue of palms and is typical of many

A farmer with the traditional all-in-one farm implement, the machete, walks along a back road in Jamaica

In pre-Revolutionary Cuba unemployment averaged 16 per cent of the labor force in 1956–1957, one of the best years of the 1950's. Even in some of the more prosperous islands, many people are out of work: in Jamaica unemployment was estimated to be 17 to 25 per cent in 1965; in Trinidad the figure was 15 per cent; and in the Netherlands Antilles, 23 per cent. In the rural areas, too, many of the plantation workers resent their seasonal unemployment and their low wages.

But there is not much work available for these people. The population density of the islands is generally high; in Barbados there are 1,398 persons per square mile; in Puerto Rico, 687. And several other islands are almost as crowded.

The situation is often worse than these figures suggest. In Haiti, for example, there are 415 persons per square mile over the whole country, but most people live in the lowlands of this mountainous country; there, the population density is close to 1,500 persons per square mile. Adding to this already large population is the high birth rate in the Caribbean, which increases the number of people and decreases job possibilities. The unemployment and the large populations are some of the causes of

182

the low income per person in the Caribbean. Annual income per person in Haiti is below $85. For many other islands it is less than $300; and the highest incomes are $700 for Puerto Rico and $900 for the Netherlands Antilles. We may compare these figures to the United States per capita income of $2,323 in 1961.

Many people leave their islands in search of work elsewhere, hoping always to return but not always achieving this hope. West Indians helped to build the Panama Canal and worked the banana plantations of Costa Rica and Honduras. Many Jamaicans went to work in Cuba during the expansion of the sugar plantations there in the last decades of the nineteenth century. For many years, and especially during World War II, workers left the smaller islands, particularly St. Vincent and Grenada, to seek work in the oil refineries of Curaçao and Aruba; some went also to Trinidad to find employment on United States military bases. This migration to Trinidad gave rise to many a calypso such as the following:

> Small island, go back where you really come from.
> You come to Trinidad in a fishing boat;
> Now you wearing a saga coat.
> Small island, go back where you really come from.

West Indians have also migrated further from home, to England and to the United States. Jamaican migration to England was as high as 39,203 in 1961, before the Commonwealth Immigrants Act of 1962 cut down the number. In 1964, however, 9,560 Jamaicans migrated to England. Jamaicans moved also to the United States, many to settle in New York City, others to seek work on farms. In 1945, 25,153 people were recruited under the Agricultural Workers Scheme, and even with more restrictive postwar immigration policies, the number continues to be high—as many as 11,542 workers came to the United States in 1964. Puerto Ricans came to the United States in even greater numbers, reaching a record high of 75,000 in 1953; since then, this migration has lessened somewhat and some people have begun to return to their island. People from the crowded island of Barbados have migrated to

183

all parts of the world. It is a standing joke in the Caribbean that when the first spaceman lands on the moon he will be met there by a Barbadian, who will greet him with a "Hoy, marn."

So we see that in spite of the "beauty and conveniency" of these Caribbean Islands, many people leave to seek better fortunes abroad. They feel that they must be able to find somewhere a better life than their poverty-stricken existence in the West Indies. But why does this poverty exist and persist amid such apparent natural bounty? The answers to this question are as abundant as the problems which beset the economy of the Caribbean.

Resources and Products

The islands have some natural resources and agricultural products; but the environment presents several difficulties. From the harbor at Port-au-Prince one has a breathtakingly beautiful view of the Haitian hills rising from the sea; but here, as in the other mountainous islands of the Caribbean, it is difficult or impossible to cultivate the steep slopes, especially when the land pattern blocks off rainfall from the leeward side of the hills.

Jamaica is a land of sparkling waterfalls, tumbling down to the valleys and shores. But here, and in many other islands, the falls prevent navigation of the rivers; and the flow of water is often too irregular to provide the hydroelectric power that would be so useful to industry. The soils of the islands, which support the luxuriant tropical vegetation, do not generally contain the combination of minerals that traditionally forms the basis for industrial development. Except for the oil and natural gas of Trinidad and the unexploited coal deposits of Haiti, few mineral fuels are known to exist in the Caribbean. The few mineral resources that have been developed tend to be those mined and exported as raw materials, so that the islands receive none of the economic benefits of mineral processing. (Curaçao has been exporting about 100,000 tons of calcium phosphate yearly.) The outstanding example is Jamaica, which exports a much greater quantity of bauxite as ore than as alumina (a processed concentrate), although the revenue received from the two

184

Two youths bathe below Annandale Falls, Grenada

exports is now almost equal, since a ton of alumina has a higher value than a ton of bauxite ore. But Jamaica still does not produce any of the final product, aluminum, which would bring a still greater revenue.

The Caribbean Islands do have assets in the fine climate and generally rich soils. But this has been a mixed blessing. The ease of growing agricultural products invited the colonial exploitation which to this day keeps the West Indian economies dependent on markets in Europe or America. The most profitable venture for an early colonist was a plantation, usually of sugar cane, supplemented by fruits, coffee, cacao, and spices. He found a ready demand for these exotic tropical foods in the European countries, and with the proceeds from his exports he imported from Europe any manufactured goods or supplementary foods that he needed. This system became a pattern of life in most of the Caribbean Islands, and it persists in their economies today.

The system of monoculture has many dangers. Because so many people are employed in its cultivation, harvesting, and trade, the fortunes of a whole country rise and fall with fluctuations in production and price of a single crop. Even under normal circumstances, this dependence on agriculture means a large amount of seasonal unemployment. Worse yet, the whole crop may be destroyed in some seasons by disease or drought or by the hurricanes that regularly menace the West Indies. In 1964–1965 thousands of people in Antigua faced economic disaster until freak rainfalls broke the drought that threatened to ruin the sugar harvest.

A particularly large crop can also bring economic difficulty, if it helps to contribute to a surplus on the world market. For, although sugar and other agricultural products are most important to the West Indies, the islands are each too small to have any control over the prices of their products abroad. They can only produce as much as possible and hope for a good price. The hope is not always, or even often, fulfilled. Low prices persist today: in 1965 Jamaica received less in payment for her sugar and banana exports than the cost of producing them.

Other Kinds of Dependence

There are four areas of the Caribbean that have escaped dependence on a single agricultural crop, but they exhibit other kinds of dependence. Jamaica, as we have seen, derives almost 50 per cent of her export revenue from bauxite or alumina. She depends heavily on mining of a single raw material; furthermore, all Jamaican bauxite exports go to the United States, so that any adverse event in American-Jamaican economic or political relations could seriously damage the Jamaican economy.

Puerto Rico, which is often cited as the great success story of the Caribbean, has indeed achieved remarkable diversity in her economy. In 1962 sugar made up only about 13 per cent of her exports, along with machinery, tobacco, clothing, and a variety of other products. But Puerto Rico depends on the United States to buy some 96 per cent of these exports and to supply 90 per cent of Puerto Rican imports, including such vital items as food, fuel, machinery, and manufacturing inputs.

186

Finally, Trinidad and the Netherlands Antilles have access to oil; but in their cases, oil becomes a sort of monoculture. Petroleum and petroleum products make up 99 per cent of the exports of Curaçao and Aruba; and the petroleum industry employs over 50 per cent of the labor force. But the islands themselves do not have oil; they import it to refine in their plants, so that some 88 per cent of their imports is crude oil from Venezuela. Trinidad has oil of her own, which she refines for domestic use and export; petroleum and its products made up 85 per cent of exports in 1962. But Trinidad also needs crude oil from Venezuela to supplement her own dwindling reserves; crude petroleum accounted for 45 per cent of imports in 1962. In addition, Trinidad imports some foodstuffs and motor vehicles.

Dependence on outside countries thus exists all through the Caribbean. For many years the Cuban economy was tied to the American market; and in her attempt to escape this dependence, Cuba found herself relying heavily on communist countries. Haiti's economy depends upon the export earnings of a few big foreign-owned firms. The British islands look to the United Kingdom for most of their trade. For example, in 1962, Barbados sent 51 per cent of its exports to Britain. The French island of Guadeloupe carries on almost 90 per cent of its trade with the franc area. Martinique gets 76 per cent of its imports

Pitch Lake, one of Trinidad's most important natural resources, is about three miles in circumference and 285 feet deep. Sir Walter Raleigh caulked his ships with pitch from the lake

A barrel conveyor from Pitch Lake
simplifies the task of loading freighters.
In this century Trinidad has supplied
15 million tons of asphalt for streets
from Lake Shore Drive in Chicago to
the Champs Elysées in Paris

from France and sends almost all its exports there. At times such dependence can force action that is harmful to the island: in 1964 living costs rose abruptly in Martinique, partly because she was obliged by France to raise tariffs against countries that did not belong to the European Economic Community—this includes neighboring Caribbean islands.

But perhaps the worst feature of the monocultures of the Caribbean is that they offer no way out of the present economic dilemma. The islands must import to live, and even in the absence of particular disasters they continually run a deficit in their balance of trade, since they spend more on imports than they receive for their exports.

Plans for Economic Independence

The Caribbean faces the unhappy situation of having to import food into one of the best agricultural climates in the world, to import fish onto islands in the middle of a sea, to import man-made goods into economies beset with unemployment. Perhaps this was acceptable during the time when the islands existed only as sources of exotic goods for colonial empires. Today, with political independence achieved or close at hand, the countries of the Caribbean are seeking ways to diversify their economies so that independence will become a reality.

"The short-term goals of the First and Second Five-Year Plans have been, and are, the freeing of the human and economic resources from their dependence on direction from abroad and the initiation of that economic and social transformation which will enable the country to realize its full potential." This is the statement of the government of Trinidad and Tobago, but it expresses the goals of all the islands in the Caribbean. In all the islands the governments have begun planning to achieve these aims because they realize that transformation must occur in a great many sectors of the economies and that they must try to hasten and coordinate changes in agriculture, industry, trade, and public services.

In agriculture there is need for increased land reform, so that more land may be made available for mixed farming, including local foods

189

and livestock. Although this might reduce the production of export crops, it would help to relieve the seasonal unemployment of one-crop plantation work and would increase the food supply of the islands, allowing them to cut down on food imports. Along with land reform, there must be better farming practices: crop rotation, increased use of fertilizers, erosion control, and more mechanization where possible, such as on cooperative farms and plantations. These better practices will increase agricultural output and will require market boards and marketing cooperatives to collect and distribute the produce efficiently, so that the farmers will receive a steady, equitable income and the whole populations of the islands will have a supply of food.

As plantation lands decrease and farming methods improve, there will be fewer people needed for agricultural production, so there will be the danger of increased unemployment, which can only be relieved by greater activity in other sectors of the economy to provide more job opportunities. Government plans try to establish, or encourage the establishment of, new manufacturing industries to process more of the

A sufficiently large quantity of pineapple is grown in Jamaica to supply both the local and foreign markets

Women porters carry banana stalks in a plastic covering from the warehouses to lighters which, in turn, carry them out to a waiting freighter

raw materials and agricultural products of the islands and to produce many basic light manufactured goods that are now imported. Such developments would improve the trade patterns of the islands; they would be able to export processed goods, which have a higher value than raw products, and they would be able to spend a greater part of their foreign earnings on the heavy machinery which they cannot produce themselves and which forms the basis for further economic development. In addition, the increased industrial activity at home would provide more jobs.

Even with coordinated planning these developments will not be automatic or easy. Adjustments among various parts of the economy

191

will lag, unemployment may increase, and people will become more impatient. In the face of protest from labor unions, governments may have to revise their plans or impose stricter controls. In Trinidad, labor unrest and strikes reached such dimensions that the government passed an Industrialization Stabilization Act making strikes illegal. Labor and management must now take their disagreements to a public court which hands down final decisions. And in Jamaica, during 1965–1966, a bitter dispute broke out between the Trade Unions and the West Indies Sugar Company. The company stated that it would be able to afford to fulfill union demands for higher wages only if it could import a mechanical harvester to cut down its costs of operation. The unions, fearing the unemployment resulting from mechanization, refused to accept this solution. Eventually the Jamaican government, under pressure from the unions, refused permission for the company to import any machinery, a decision that must retard development in the long run, although it may be the only possible way to prevent greater unemployment and poverty in the short run.

In a more positive way, governments plan to improve the living conditions of their peoples and to provide increased employment through projects to improve public services in the islands, to provide pure water, electricity, sewer systems, roads, and medical services, which are lacking in so many of the poorer communities. In an effort to develop the human resources of the islands, the governments devote a large part of their resources to education and training. The great problem facing Caribbean planners is the limited size of the government budgets; and the task before them is to increase their revenues or to direct private revenues so as to bring about economic growth in the islands. As we look briefly at the economic plans of the Caribbean, we shall see some of the ways in which the islands have tried to solve this problem.

Puerto Rico

Puerto Rico has been economically fortunate in her ties to the United States. Anxious to have a showplace of democracy in the Caribbean, the United States has been generous in technical and financial aid to Puerto Rico to bring about land reform and to establish such basic services as electric power and water supply, public housing, hospitals, and vocational education. Once development was under way, American businessmen were glad to invest in this American-controlled island which offered prospects of low labor costs and safe, high profits.

The great part of the credit for Puerto Rico's remarkable economic development, however, goes to the Puerto Ricans themselves, whose own personal efforts to improve their condition have become known as "Operation Bootstrap." Governor Muñoz Marín and other government leaders set out to talk to the people of Puerto Rico, to find out their needs, and to help them work toward solving these problems themselves. Perhaps the best example of this self-help is the housing program.

One of the many supermarkets opened in Puerto Rico in recent years in the wake of higher living standards resulting from "Operation Bootstrap." A large sign urges in Spanish "Use products of your country"

The government lends to a community a concrete block-making machine and a cement mixer. Using materials furnished by the government, the people build their own houses. During the next ten years each owner must repay the government for the materials, but in the meantime he has his own house, with space for a garden of flowers and vegetables.

People also have a greater chance for economic independence because of the government land reform and industrialization programs. The smaller farmers, freed from control by large landowners, receive income from the sale of their own sugar cane, coffee, tobacco, and fruit. Processing of these agricultural products provides work for many of the townspeople; and in addition, many other kinds of light industry, including branches of American manufacturing concerns, have established themselves in Puerto Rico. There they can take advantage of the lower taxes which the government allows for new industries; and they can find workers among the increasingly skilled labor force of the island.

The rising income makes possible some market for manufactured goods in Puerto Rico. The island also has special access to the huge market in the United States; and tourists from her big northern neighbor play an important part in the Puerto Rican economy. The most recent economic plans include even greater expansion of the tourist industry; but the government is also trying to improve the inner development of the island by giving special benefits to manufacturers who set up factories in less-developed areas and by encouraging increased farming of livestock, poultry, fruits, and vegetables.

Haiti and the Dominican Republic

Other islands have not been so fortunate as Puerto Rico in their economic leadership or foreign aid. Haiti and the Dominican Republic especially have suffered from exploitation by dictators and from foreign intervention and control of their economies. In Haiti the economy has declined rather than improved in recent years. Under President Duvalier's rigid control and corrupt administration, economic planning seems most concerned with preventing the growth of any private Haitian

194

businessmen. Instead, the economy remains in the control of big foreign firms that supply revenue for the Haitian government while they divert the country's resources to their own use. While the Haitian people remain miserably poor, either foreign monopolies or the state controls the export of agricultural products and raw materials and the import of manufactured goods. American firms handle production of sugar, flour, sisal, copper, bauxite, beef, and other goods. At the same time the successful Haitian enterprises have been seized by the government.

In the Dominican Republic the dictator Rafael Trujillo did develop the country's economy somewhat, even while he enriched himself. He left behind him a good road system and some fine public buildings and parks, as well as vast agricultural and industrial properties he had assembled for his own. But most of the Dominican people remained dependent on subsistence farming while the country as a whole depended on the export of agricultural products.

Trujillo's assassination resulted in political chaos that has prevented improvement of the economy and has postponed decisions on how to use the Trujillo property, which is now held by the state. With large amounts of financial aid from the United States, the national product grew at a slow rate from 1961 to 1965, although much of the growth went into increased consumption by the upper classes, often made possible by smuggling goods into the country. In 1965 export income decreased because of difficulties in marketing sugar, coffee, cocoa, and tobacco; businesses ran at a loss, and at least 30 per cent of the labor force was unemployed. Now, open civil war has brought the country close to complete economic collapse.

Perhaps the greatest tragedy of these two countries is that they share an island that is potentially one of the richest in the Caribbean. It possesses unexploited mineral resources and hydroelectric power and a fine climate which produces a good coffee crop in Haiti and which has enabled the Dominican farmers usually to support themselves well in spite of the political unrest around them. And most of all, the island has the unexploited human resources of people who have never had a chance to develop themselves in security and peace.

Workers cutting sugar cane in Puerto Rico. The cane is first set on fire to burn away the excess foliage, making it easier to cut

Cuba

Cuba, too, is a naturally rich island. Here, also, for many years the welfare of the people was sacrificed to the interests of dictators and dependence on agricultural exports; in this case the one crop, sugar, was sold almost entirely to one country, the United States.

The Cuban Revolution of 1959 drove out the dictator Batista, and the new government has been trying to reduce the island's dependence on sugar and to eliminate unemployment, poverty, and illiteracy within

196

a few years. The results of this ambitious program have been mixed. Without doubt, the distribution of income is more equal in Cuba now than it was before the Revolution. The land reform forbade ownership of large estates, which were taken over by the government to be distributed to small farmers or to be operated as cooperatives or state farms.

In 1961 the small farmers joined together in a nationwide association to coordinate their production with the national program. New areas were brought under cultivation using improved techniques, and rural employment increased. These areas were planted with new crops, such as rice, cotton, peanuts, potatoes, and soybeans, rather than the traditional sugar, coffee, and tobacco. In this way the government hoped to reduce food imports. Progress in raising agricultural production has been uneven. The sugar crop of 1961 was the second largest in Cuba's history, but then production fell off until the good crop of 1965. Output of eggs, milk, meat, and some vegetables has been about the same or higher; but there have been many problems in transporting and distributing the food around the island. Also, in the rural areas the government has devoted much—perhaps too much—of its resources to improvement of education, medical clinics, housing, and public works, in order to make the life of people there a part of the national life.

The government has also planned for improvement and diversification of industrial production to develop Cuba's unused resources and to reduce imports of manufactured goods. The plans include building an iron and steel plant, which will use the large iron deposits in Oriente Province, and expanding production of the island's nickel and cobalt. Cuba plans eventually to produce her own automobiles, bicycles, railway equipment and agricultural machinery, rather than importing them. There is a new program to build fishing boats and plans for a petroleum refinery and two new electricity plants. Cuba is also engaged in chemical research to discover new uses for by-products of sugar cane and other plants of the island. In its industrial plans, the government is attempting to locate factories in various parts of the island so that development will take place throughout the country.

The Cuban leaders have not so far accomplished all that they hoped for; but their goals were unrealistic in the face of such serious problems. Most of the failures have occurred in organization and adjustment of the economy to new ideas, not in the ideas themselves. Cuba seems now to have paused briefly; but the Cuban planners are working hard to correct their previous mistakes and to provide the education and training that will help the Cuban people to develop their country further.

Plans for the Other Islands

Among the other Caribbean Islands, Jamaica and Trinidad, because of their size and diversity, have the best opportunities for industrial development. For the smaller islands, which have not yet become independent, planning is directed by the metropolitan country on the basis of reports from the islands. In modern days the economic planning objectives have become about the same for these nonindependent territories as for the independent islands. The policies generally include: increasing productivity in agriculture and other traditional industries; developing new manufacturing industries to increase exports and reduce imports; improving public services such as transportation, communications, and electricity; increasing education and technical training; and developing the tourist industry.

In Guadeloupe the Forest Service is planting new valuable woods, such as mahogany, and is opening roads through the forest in order to develop forest industries. A fishing cooperative has given many loans to equip Guadeloupe's fishing fleet and has built warehouses for supplies and equipment. In Martinique, which depends heavily on sugar, banana, and pineapple exports, the Agricultural Services are encouraging farmers to plant more coffee and cacao because the trees help to prevent erosion and the products have a good market. In both islands new industries receive tax exemptions for several years.

In the Netherlands Antilles, whose economies rely almost completely on refining petroleum from Venezuela, the government is searching for local raw materials that will provide a basis for industry. Large deposits of calcium phosphate in Aruba will be used in the island's chemical plants, which already produce a number of chemicals for fertilizers. Aruba has a plant to distill sea water, the largest of its kind in the world. Along with fresh water, the plant yields some raw materials for use in the chemical industries. In both Curaçao and Aruba, the government encourages building of shops and hotels which will enhance the islands' natural attractions for tourists.

The smaller British islands have programs for general development, such as the current five-year plan of Grenada, which calls for improvement in agriculture, water resources, roads, tourist promotion, and school facilities. The islands also encourage particular industrial developments such as the new oil refinery in Antigua.

The government of Trinidad and Tobago began to use economic plans before independence. From 1958 to 1962 Trinidad had a five-year program to provide basic services, such as communications, water,

Flying fish are sold from the boat directly to customers on the beach in Barbados. These fish are a special delicacy on the island

and electricity, that are necessary for agricultural and industrial growth. The government also worked to improve living conditions through facilities for health, education, and housing; and it tried to find jobs for Trinidad's many unemployed workers. In contrast to the Cuban approach, Trinidad hopes that agriculture and industry will grow through private enterprise. The government encourages such growth by giving subsidies for the cultivation of new crops and granting tax exemptions to new industries. Also, the Industrial Development Corporation improves land for industrial use and helps new factories to get started. Since independence, Trinidad has a Second Five-Year Plan for 1964 to 1968, which continues the same general policies but stresses even further that the country needs to get away from dependence on trade of petroleum and sugar. The government is encouraging farmers to produce meat and vegetables as food for the people of Trinidad; and it is aiding businessmen to start new manufacturing industries that will make products for the local market and for export. In 1965 several new industries were begun, including a shoe factory, a flour mill, and an automobile assembly plant.

Jamaica, since independence, has turned inward more than Trinidad. In 1964, for instance, a new law was passed that gives Jamaicans priority over foreigners for any available job. The Five-Year Independence Plan expects slower growth for bauxite and sugar exports; instead, it concentrates on increasing production of food and manufactured goods for Jamaican consumption and on improving social services in the country. The government has set up agricultural training centers and machinery pools to help farmers with cultivation, as well as an Agricultural Marketing Corporation to provide the best possible prices for the farmers and a continuous supply of food for consumers.

In order to encourage manufacturing, the Jamaican government gives tax exemptions to new firms and often forbids the import of goods that would compete with the products of a new manufacturer. The Jamaican Industrial Development Corporation investigates possibilities for new industry, and provides money and training to help establish factories. Plans for new industry in Jamaica include a tire factory, which will supply almost all the tires and tubes for the island, expansion of an alumina plant, and a steel mill to produce steel from local scrap metal and imported iron. The Jamaican people now seem to be willing to invest their money in new industries, providing a source of capital besides foreign aid and investment. Jamaica is also trying to improve production in existing industries by such programs as exploratory fishing and research into better methods of cultivating sugar cane.

Postscript

And so the peoples of the Caribbean plan or attempt to shape their future. But all too often these plans are upset by the untimely actions of men or by the unforeseen violence of natural forces. The former result in civil disorder and strife, the latter in the violence of destructive hurricanes. But even discounting the destructive forces of men and of natural phenomena, the given potential of the islands is so limited that new planning must utilize all the resources of the islands. The very definition of *island* means *sea*. And it is to the vast and as yet untapped resources of the sea that these small islands must look.

The land area of the islands is small, and so their capacity to produce large quantities of raw materials is extremely limited. Even large raw producing areas of the world are at the exploitive mercy of highly industrialized countries and areas whose crippling trade directives put them in a market prison. Small raw producing areas such as the Caribbean are like little fish swimming next to a whale. Even if the little fish come together they cannot compete with the whale, yet they must still continue to swim; and the islands must attempt to swim along with the whale but free of it.

Many planners are talking of Caribbean regional economic planning that would harmonize the Caribbean economies, coordinating their industry, manufacturing, trade, and tourism, and thereby creating a Caribbean community as self-sufficient as possible. The sea would serve as an avenue of trade between the islands instead of a barrier. (At

This underwater novice receives expert instruction in the art of scuba diving in the Virgin Islands where tourism is an important source of income

203

Fort San Jeronimo, built in 1788 to protect Old San Juan from British attack, contrasts with the resort hotels of the modern city

present many of the Caribbean islands trade with countries as far away as Australia, New Zealand, Syria, and China, but they hardly trade with one another.) Economic harmony between the islands would enable the Caribbean community to become a self-sufficient free-trade area where light manufactured goods produced in the islands would be marketed within the islands, thereby lessening imports from larger countries of the world. The tropical agricultural produce of the islands would be pooled together and sold on the world market. This would increase the growth of communication between the islands. For even though the islands are linked with the outside world by air routes and

204

sea lanes, there is comparatively little communication among them. The inner link between the islands is quite limited and there are few links with South America.

"And the trees run down to the sea. And the sun shines gaily on the mountain tops." And myriad stars shine like gleaming pebbles in the sky over these lovely islands. The blue-green sea reflects the blue skies when the weather is calm, or the waves ride high, smashing into the shore when the strong trade winds drive them on. But the many great harbors of the islands are sheltered from these winds, and ships of many nations ride at rest in them. Harbors which once saw the

The skill and craftsmanship of Arawaks, Caribs, and Africans has been passed down to contemporary islanders who fashion by hand fanciful woodcraft, pottery, and jewellery

The pool and terrace of a modern resort hotel at Ponce, Puerto Rico. Visitors are encouraged to discover the beauties of the island beyond San Juan

sight of admirals and pirates, of Nelson, Rodney and DeGrasse, of Drake and Morgan, and of Spanish fleets filled with bullion from the Aztec and Inca empires, now see peoples from all over the world disembark—visitors anxious to unravel the web of the islands' history with its myriad interwoven events, its many races mixing together in apparent harmony. Many of the tourists come from the temperate north—the United States and Canada—bringing with them much-needed capital and creating a tourist trade on which many Caribbean

206

economies count for a good measure of their capital. The tourists come to enjoy the music, dance, and song of the islands. They wonder at the growth of the cultural life of the islands and at the existence of the many theatrical groups and dance troupes, and the painting and sculpture and ceramics of many young Caribbean artists. The tourists are puzzled by the signs of a low standard of living in the islands so close to their own shores.

Even as these visitors bring some revenue to the islands' budgets, they display such affluence that many of the island people reject their island attitudes and attempt, unfortunately, to pattern their lives after people from highly urban industrial societies. The many outward trappings of affluence displayed by the tourists incense the minds of the

A fisherman of Martinique speaks French and makes his living in the same way as his ancestors

A skilled worker in an electronics plant at Ponce. Puerto Rico has a program to encourage foreign manufacturers to come to the island

islanders, who forget that they are island people whose potential for an industrial society is limited.

The tourists revel in the recreational possibilities of the sea—swimming, boating, water skiing, surfing, and exploring the wealth of marine life offered by the Caribbean Sea. But as yet the peoples of the Caribbean do not appreciate the full possibilities of the sea around them. They do not fully realize the possibility of relaxation and enjoyment of sport and exercise which the sea offers them: many of the island peoples have never learned to swim.

As yet the departments of fisheries of the islands and the research into the development of fisheries do not form a very vital part of the economic planning of the islands. While Cuba exports lobsters to Syria and Jamaica imports salt fish for its national dish, the sea around the islands abounds in fish and marine life that, with proper fishing methods, could form a valuable source of revenue for the islands and food for their peoples. As yet few industries have been developed to process marine weeds and plant life which form the basis of many products. As yet the islands import fish oils, fish foods, fish fertilizer, and have not yet turned to producing these things for themselves.

The sea offers the Caribbean planners an exciting area of investigation and development. Fish-processing and boat-building industries could bring about increased revenue and lessen unemployment. The recreational possibilities of the sea could help to absorb the amazing vitality of peoples who live in the small land areas.

Men in Barbados mend sails. Fishing could become an important industry in the West Indies

Today many people in the Caribbean Islands are going deep within themselves to create an island culture, to develop art, literature, and painting, to harmonize the islands' music and dance with the stream of world cultures so that songs of the islands may be heard.

The problems facing the peoples of the Caribbean are many; but they plan and plan. They hope for good government and wise rulers who will not smother the fires of dissent but will use their skill to prevent the destructive chaos of revolution. They hope for wise economic planning which will use in concert and to the full the limited resources of the islands, which will control the high population growth

Floats make their way through gaily decorated Kingston on the occasion of Jamaica's second anniversary of independence

and institute good social services, and which will tap the vast resources of the sea. They wait, these peoples, for an education that will unite them with the total rhythm of their lands and give them a knowledge and feel of the sea around them and a sense and grasp of international concerns.

The island peoples dream of making their tropical green islands wonderful places for living. And the Caribbean peoples, shaped by the movement of their diversified history and rocked by the rhythms of their culture, pursue their dreams.

Other Books to Enjoy

NON-FICTION

Buccaneers of America, by John Esquemeling. New York: Dover, 1966. (Paperback)

Black Fire: Henri Christophe, by Covelle Newcomb. New York: McKay, 1940.

Christopher Columbus, Mariner, by Samuel Eliot Morison. New York: New American Library, 1956. (Paperback)

Citizen Toussaint, by Ralph Korngold. New York: Hill & Wang, 1965. (Paperback)

Crossroads of Conquerors, by F. Wenderoth Saunders. Boston: Little, Brown, 1962.

Cuba, Haiti, and the Dominican Republic, by John E. Fagg. New York: Prentice-Hall, 1965. (Paperback)

Puerto Rico: Island of Promise, by Ruth Gruber. New York: Hill & Wang, 1960.

Standard Guide to the Caribbean, by Lawrence and Sylvia Martin. New York: Funk & Wagnalls. (Paperback)

West Indies, by P.M. Sherlock. New York: Walker, 1966.

Young People of the West Indies, by Charles R. Joy. New York: Meredith, 1964.

Young Traveler in the West Indies, by Lucille Iremonger. New York: Dutton, 1955.

FICTION

Anansi, the Spider Man, by Philip M. Sherlock. New York: Crowell, 1954.

Drought, by Andrew Salkey. London: Oxford Univ. Press, 1966.

From the Green Antilles, selections from the literature edited by Barbara Howes. New York: Macmillan, 1966.

Hurricane, by Andrew Salkey. London: Oxford Univ. Press, 1964.

Jamaican Song and Story, by Walter Jekyll. New York: Dover, 1966. (Paperback)

Piece of Fire, and other Haitian Tales, by Harold Courlander. New York: Harcourt, 1964.

Three-finger Jack's Treasure, by Philip M. Sherlock. New York: St. Martins, 1961.

West Indian Folk Tales, by Philip M. Sherlock. New York: Walck, 1966.

Highlights in West Indian History

1492   Columbus arrives at the island of Guanahani in the Bahamas, and the New World is discovered by Europeans

1494   Papal Bull awards Spain dominion over the West Indies

1509   Ponce de León arrives in Puerto Rico with first Spanish settlers

1518   Spanish crown begins to grant licences to private traders for import of slaves into the West Indies

1562   Jack Hawkin's first voyage which anticipated the triangle trade whereby slaves were brought from Africa, sugar and other West Indian products were transported to England, and thereby traders were provided with textiles and other goods to trade for African slaves

1585   Drake's "Indies Voyage" emphasizes the importance of the West Indies to European rivalries

1604   James I of England declares that he is not prepared to respect Spanish rights in unoccupied parts of America

1624   First permanent English settlement in the West Indies begins in St. Christopher

1627   British occupy Barbados

1635   Settlement of Martinique and Guadeloupe by the French

1637   First sugarcane brought from Brazil and planted in Barbados, marking the beginning of sugar as an important commercial crop

1648   Dutch possession of Curaçao, St. Martin, and St. Eustatius confirmed by Treaty of Münster

1649   First serious mutiny of slaves, in Barbados

1685   The *Code Noir,* promulgated by Louis XIV of France, reflects the government's determination to prevent slave insurrections due to the irresponsibility of the owners

1697   Treaty of Ryswick cedes St. Domingue (Haiti) to France

1713   Treaty of Utrecht provides that Dutch and Spanish America will not fall under French domination, and transfers some trading

214

	rights in Spanish America to a concern established for that purpose
1739	War of Jenkins' Ear, between England and Spain, the first major European war fought expressly over West Indies trade
1776	British West Indians opt for supporting Britain rather than the North American colonies during the War of Independence
1791	First, concerted, large-scale slave revolt occurs in the French island of St. Domingue.
1792	Denmark is the first country to abolish the slave trade
1804	Dessalines proclaims Haiti, formerly St. Domingue, an independent country
1808	Passage of the Abolition of the Slave Trade Act in England at a time when over one half the trade was in British hands
1833	Emancipation Act for the British West Indies is passed
1848	Slavery abolished in French West Indies
1846	Beginning of East Indian migration into Trinidad
1898	Spanish-American War. In the Caribbean it results in the U.S. occupation of Cuba for three years and the annexation of Puerto Rico by the United States
1904	U.S. President Theodore Roosevelt enunciates the "corollary" to the Monroe Doctrine
1906–9	United States occupies Cuba after Estrada Palma, faced with a revolt upon his election, resigns
1915–34	United States occupies Haiti after a president is ousted in a "revolution"
1916–24	Military occupation of Santo Domingo by United States
1930	General Rafael Trujillo comes into power in Santo Domingo
1933	Machado, the Cuban dictator, is overthrown, and Batista rises to power for the first time
1940	Popular Democratic Party in Puerto Rico gains power, marking the beginning of "Operation Bootstrap"
1947	Jamaica House of Representatives elected for the first time by full adult suffrage, signalling the beginning of the movement for self-government
1949	Charter granted to the University of the West Indies
1952	Puerto Rico becomes a commonwealth under the aegis of the United States

1958	First elections for the newly formed Federation of the West Indies, climaxing discussions which began in 1947
1958–9	Batista driven from office in Cuba primarily through the 26th of July Movement, headed by Dr. Fidel Castro
1961	Jamaica votes against Federation and withdraws. Subsequently the West Indies Federation collapses. The Bay of Pigs invasion by exiled Cubans fails
1962	Jamaica, Trinidad, and Tobago achieve independence. The Soviet Union removes missile installations from Cuba after a direct confrontation by President Kennedy and a mercantile blockade of the island
1965	The ruling civilian junta in the Dominican Republic is overthrown, and an Inter-American military force takes over the country with the approval of the OAS
1966	Barbados achieves independence

Index

Adams, Grantley, 167
Africa and the Africans, 17, 29, 33, 34, 37, 39, 40, 41, 42, 46, 47, 50, 52, 53, 61, 82, 90. *See also* Slavery
Agriculture, 73, 104, 131, 155, 157, 180, 184, 186, 189, 190, 200, 204. *See also* Farms and Farming; Crops
American Revolution, 81, 87. *See also* United States
Amis de Noir, 87
Anglican Religion, 38
Anguilla, 19, 168
Antigua, 19, 20, 72, 168, 186
Antilles,
　　Greater, 18, 20
　　Lesser, 18, 19, 20
Arawaks, 16, 17, 35, 68, 118, 205
Arias, President, 114
Arts and Crafts, 134–135, 210
Aruba, 16, 46–47, 173–175, 183, 199
Ashanti, 82
Ashburton Treaty, 90
Asia and the Asians, 34
Australia, 204

Bahamas, 16
Baptists, 39
Barbados, 20, 21, 70, 71, 85, 138, 141, 181, 209
　　climate, 22, 25
　　education, 120
　　government, 165–173
　　illiteracy, 128
　　language, 46
　　music, 49
　　religion, 38
　　settlement, 72
　　unemployment, 182, 183
Bataka, 36

Batista, Fulgencio, 108, 151, 152, 153, 154, 196
Battle of the Saintes, 80
Bay of Pigs Invasion, 155, 156
Balaguer, Juaquin, 157
Bermudas, 15
Betancourt, Romulo, 157
Bligh, Captain William, 79
Bonaire, 16
Bonaparte, Napoleon, 72, 73, 86, 88
Bosch, Juan, 157
Boukman, 88
Bridgetown, 70
Buccaneering, 69, 72, 74–75, 77
Bustamente, Alexander, 167
Butler, Uriah, 167

Calypso, 48, 49, 50, 51, 56–57. *See also* Entertainment
Campbell, George, 30
Canada, 134, 206
Caperton, Admiral, 110
Cap Hatien, 86
Caribs, 16, 17, 35, 36, 68, 72, 118, 205
Casals, Pablo, 103
Castro, Fidel, 129, 152, 153, 154, 155, 156
Castro, Raul, 153
Cecil, Sir William, 65
Charles V, Emperor, 67
China and the Chinese, 17, 91, 204
Christophe, Henri, 86, 88, 89
Church of God, 39
Cipriani, Arthur, 167
Ciudad Trujillo (Santo Domingo), 98, 157
Climate, 18, 22–26, 178, 185, 189
Code Noir, 84
Codrington College, Barbados, 120, 135. *See also* Education

Columbus, Christopher, 11–18, 24, 60, 61, 62, 177. *See also* Exploration
Commonwealth Immigrants Act (1962), 183
Congregationalists, 39
Conquistadores, 62
Coromantines, 82
Creole, 36, 45–46, 52, 101, 131–132. *See also* Language; Races
Crops, 13, 21, 25, 29, 76, 82–84, 88, 91, 92–94, 102–103, 107–108, 151, 177, 185, 186, 190, 194, 197
Crowder, General, 108
Crowley, Daniel J., 30, 57, 58, 59
Cuba, 18, 20, 92, 98, 101–102, 125, 152, 153, 209
  agriculture, 132
  climate, 24
  discovery, 61
  education, 136
  government, 104–109
  illiteracy, 128–130
  industry, 93–94
  language, 45
  literature, 144–146
  religion, 37, 40, 42
  resources, 196–198
  revolution and aftermath, 151–156
  settlement, 63
  song and dance, 50
  Spanish-U.S. War, 99–100, 103
  unemployment, 182
Cuba Revolution, 125, 154, 196–198
Cumina, 39
Curacao, 74, 172, 174, 183, 199
  education, 119
  government, 173–175
  heritage, 36
  language, 46–47
  religion, 37–38
  resources, 184, 187
  settlement, 72
Customs and Beliefs (Folklore), 34, 50, 52, 147. *See also* Religion

Dance, 49–50
De Grasse, Commander, 80, 206

Denmark and the Danish, 29, 90. *See also* Virgin Islands
d'Esnambuc, 72
Dessalines, Jean Jacques, 88
Dominica, 17, 19, 20, 168, 179
  climate, 22
  religion, 37
Dominican Republic, 18, 97, 98, 104, 126
  government, 109, 111–114
  illiteracy, 128
  heritage, 36
  language, 45–46
  religion, 37
  revolution, 156–158
  song and dance, 49–50
Drake, Sir Francis, 69, 206
Duvalier, François, 160, 161, 194

East Indians, 42, 47, 52
Economics, 92–94, 98, 107–108, 110, 115, 151, 155, 161, 178, 186, 187, 193, 194, 195, 203. *See also* Trade; Crops; Agriculture; Industry
Education, 118, 120–123, 125, 126, 128, 129, 132, 135, 139
Eisenhower, President, 155
Emancipation Act of England, 90
England and the English, 15, 29, 45, 46, 47, 65, 66, 67, 71, 72, 73, 75, 76, 78–79, 80, 81, 82, 84, 89, 90, 94, 117, 118–119, 125, 165–173, 183, 187
Entertainment, 49, 134, 147, 180, 208
Estime, Dumarsais, 159
Europe and the Europeans, 17, 27, 29, 35, 39, 42, 49, 62, 66, 69, 74, 81, 89, 97, 99, 111, 178, 181, 189
European Economic Community, 189
Exploration, 11–15, 61–63
Exports, 178, 190, 195, 200, 209

Faces of Love, The, 142
Farms and farming, 190, 194. *See also* Agriculture
Federation (of B.W.I.), 170–173
Ferdinand and Isabella (of Spain), 12, 61

Festivals and carnivals, 39, 52–53, 55–56, 58

Fishing, 97, 146, 179–180, 199, 209. *See also* Trade

Food, 34, 53, 177, 180, 185, 189

Fort of France, 44

Fountain of Youth, 15

Fouché, Franck, 147

France and the French, 15, 29, 37, 38, 43, 44, 45, 46, 47, 49, 50, 53, 55, 65, 66, 67, 69, 71, 72, 73, 75, 76, 78–79, 80, 81, 84, 87–88, 94, 117, 118–119, 125, 173–175, 207

Francis I (of France), 65

French Revolution, 87

Geography, 18–21, 26–27, 120, 131, 177, 184, 209. *See also* Climate; Crops

Goveia, Elsa, 85, 91

Government and constitution, 76–77, 78, 94, 99, 100, 103, 104–105, 108, 115, 151, 152, 158–159, 161, 162–166, 168–171, 174–175

Grenada, 19, 21, 67, 168, 171, 179, 183, 185, 199

Guadeloupe, 73, 125
   education, 118–119, 120, 122
   government, 94, 173–175
   heritage, 36
   language, 46
   religion, 37
   resources, 187, 189
   song and dance, 50

Guevara, Che, 154

Guillén, Nicolás, 144–146

Haiti, 18, 82, 89, 97, 104, 159. *See also* St. Domingue
   agriculture, 131–132
   education, 119, 136, 139
   government, 109–111, 114
   independence, 88
   language, 46
   literature, 147
   religion, 37, 40, 42
   resources, 184, 194–195
   revolution, 158–161

   song and dance, 49–50
   unemployment, 182–183

Hawkins, John, 66

Havana, 18, 100

Hein, Peter, 73

Hearne, John, 142–144

Hispaniola, 18, 20, 68
   discovery, 61
   settlement, 63

Holland and the Dutch, 15, 19, 36, 38, 46, 47, 69, 71, 72, 73, 76, 81, 82, 117, 173–175

Ibo, 39, 82

Illiteracy, 128, 129, 152. *See also* Education

Imperial College of Tropical Agriculture, Trinidad, 120, 135. *See also* Crops; Education

Imports, 186, 209

Industrialization Stabilization Act (Trinidad), 192

In the Castle of my Skin, 141

Indians, 17, 29, 32, 34, 35, 46, 47, 52–53, 61, 62, 68, 91, 92. *See also* East Indians

Industry, 99, 145, 151, 155, 197–201, 207–208, 209. *See also* Economics

Jamaica, 18, 26, 61, 71, 75, 78, 84, 117, 121, 124, 135, 146, 179–181, 190, 192, 198, 200–201, 209, 210
   climate, 22
   education, 137–139
   festivals, 52
   food, 177
   government, 165–173
   heritage, 36
   illiteracy, 128
   language, 46
   music, 49–50
   religion, 38–40
   resources, 184–186
   unemployment, 182–183
   youth, 130–131

Jamaica Youth Corps, 131

Jehovah's Witnesses, 39

Jiménez, President, 114

John II (of Portugal), 61
John Canoe Festival, 52–53
Josephine, Empress (Rose Josephine De La Pagène), 72, 73
Judaism and Jews, 37, 38

Kingston, 130, 137, 138

Labor (work), 127, 161, 182, 192, 195. *See also* Racial Characteristics; Races; Unemployment
Lamming, George, 141
Land, 142, 143
Language, 45–47, 117, 119, 128, 131, 132. *See also* individual languages; Education
Las Casas, de, Bartolomeo, 69, 75
Le Clerc, François, 66
Leeward Islands, 18, 67, 168, 173
Lescot, Elie, 158
Levasseur, 75
Limbo, 50–51
Linstead, 177, 180
Literature, 15, 30, 32–33, 47, 57, 58–59, 141, 142–144, 145–147, 148–149. *See also* Writers
London, 38, 50, 172
Lutherans, 39

McKay, Claude, 148
Machado, Gerardo, 108
Magloire, Colonel Paul, 159, 160
Maine (battleship), 100
Mandingo, 39, 82
Manley, Norman, 167
Margaret, Princess, 166
Marín, Muñoz, Governor, 161, 162, 163, 193
Maroons, 36
Marryshow, T. M., 167
Martí, José, 99, 101, 129
Martinique, 21, 44, 45, 72, 73, 125, 207
  constitution, 94
  education, 118–119, 120, 122
  government, 173–175
  language, 46
  religion, 37, 40

resources, 187, 189
song and dance, 49–50
Methodists, 39
Mexico, 20, 24, 62, 153
Midnight Robbers, The, 58
Migration, 156, 183. *See also* Unemployment
Miguel Such Vocational School, 126. *See also* Education; Arts and Crafts
Milot, 89
Mittelholzer, Edgar, 32
Mona, 26, 137
Monroe Doctrine (1820), 97, 98, 99, 100, 112, 156, 158. *See also* United States
Montbars of Languedoc, Sieur de, 75
Montezuma, 62
Montserrat, 18, 19, 72, 168
Moravians, 39
Morgan, Henry, 69, 75, 206. *See also* Buccaneering
Morning at the Office, A, 32
Mt. Pelée, 21
Mountains, 20–21
Music, 34, 49–50, 53, 55, 56, 58
Muslims, 37, 52

Nelson, Admiral Lord, 70, 206
Nevis, 19, 72, 168
Notebook by Macaw, 47
Nutmeg tree, 179

Operation Bootstrap, 193
Organic Act of 1900, 115
Organization of American States (OAS), 156, 158

Padilla, Carlos, 147
Panama, 24
Panama Canal, 100, 183
Papal Bull, 65
Peace Corps, 92, 93, 112, 113, 127, 134
Peligre Dam, 160
Pico Turquino, 132
Pitch Lake, 187, 188. *See also* Resources
Plaisance, 11, 132
Point-à-Pitre, 37
Platt Amendment, 105, 107, 108. *See also* United States

Ponce, 206, 208
Ponce de León, 63
Population, 182–183. *See also* Races; Racial Characteristics
Port-au-Prince, 184
Port-of-Spain, 57, 167
Port Royal, 18, 34, 57, 69, 75
Portugal and the Portuguese, 61, 82, 90
Powell, John, 72
Presbyterians, 39
Protestants, 38
Puerto Rico, 18, 20, 22, 37, 62, 63, 64, 94, 125, 126, 128, 162, 163, 175, 208
  climate, 24
  education, 122, 136
  government, 105–106, 114–115, 161–165
  heritage, 35
  illiteracy, 128–130
  literature, 147
  people, 102–103
  resources, 186, 192–194
  song and dance, 49–50
  unemployment, 182–183

Quakers, 38

Races, 16, 17, 29–30, 33, 34–37, 46, 56, 68, 69, 82, 91, 92, 101, 103, 104. *See also* Population; Racial Characteristics
Racial Characteristics, 47, 68, 118, 123, 125, 160, 179, 180, 183, 186
Raleigh, Sir Walter, 187
Reforms, 95, 110, 114–115, 138, 160, 192, 193, 196–197, 200, 211
Religion, 34–37, 38–43, 59, 75, 89, 103. *See also* Individual Religions
Resources, 62–63, 184, 185, 186–187, 195, 197
Revolts and Revolutions, 81, 87, 88, 99, 104, 111, 114, 153–154, 155, 158
Richelieu, Cardinal, 72
Robinson Crusoe, 14, 15
Rodney, Admiral Lord, 80, 81, 206
Roman Catholics and Catholicism, 36–40, 42, 103, 118
Roosevelt, President Theodore, 112

Roosevelt Corollary, 100, 111

Saba, 20, 21, 36, 72
St. Christopher, 19, 71, 72, 168
St. Croix, 79
St. Domingue (now Haiti), 75, 79, 84, 87, 88
St. Domingue Revolution, 87, 88
St. Eustatius, 20, 72, 81
St. John, 97
St. Lucia, 17, 19, 72, 84, 92, 134, 168
  language, 45–46
  religion, 37
St. Martin, 20, 72
St. Thomas, 97
St. Vincent, 17, 23, 40, 79, 84, 168, 178, 183
Sanchez-Vilella, Roberto, 162
San Germán, 102
San Juan, 63, 77, 101, 102, 105, 163, 204, 206
San Martin, 151
San Salvador, 12, 61
Santiago, 153
Santo Domingo (Ciudad Trujillo), 98, 157
Santo Domingo University, 136, 139
Saut d'eau, 38
Savannah, The, 167
Scouts and scouting, 124
Selkirk, Alexander, 14, 15
Settlement, 72, 75, 76. *See also* Exploration
Seventh Day Adventists, 39
Seven Years' War, 80
Shakespeare, William, 11, 15
Ships and shipping, 64, 66, 71–72, 78, 99
Sierra Maestra, 132, 153
Slavery, 17, 29, 38, 69, 77, 78, 81–82, 85, 86–91, 110. *See also* Races
Socarras, 151
Song, 46, 48, 49–51, 71, 183. *See also* Entertainment
South America, 16, 17, 18, 20, 205
Spain and the Spanish, 11–15, 17, 29, 33, 37, 38, 46, 47, 53, 61, 63, 64, 65, 66, 68, 69, 71, 73, 75, 76, 80, 81, 82, 90, 94, 100, 101–106, 117, 118–119, 206

Spanish-American War, 94, 100, 106
Sport, 116, 123, 124, 167, 180, 208
Springer, H. W., 135
Stranger at the Gate, 143
Stuyvesant, Peter, 119
Superstition, 43, 44. *See also* Customs
   and Beliefs; Religion; Voodoo
Sweden, 82, 90
Syria, 29, 204

The Tempest, 11, 15
Ten-Years' War (for Cuban Nationalism),
   102
Tobacco, 178
Tobago, 14, 15, 199, 200
   climate, 24
   dances, 49
   education, 125–126
   government, 165–173
   illiteracy, 128
Tortuga, 69, 74
Toussaint L'Ouverture, Pierre Dominique,
   88
Trade, 38, 63–64, 66, 68, 72–74, 76–77,
   85, 92–94, 98, 101–102, 107–108, 147,
   187, 189, 191, 195
Traditional Masques of Carnival, 57, 59
Treasure Island, 13, 16
Treaty of General Relations, 109
Treaty of Ryswick, 76
Treaty of Ratisbon, 76
Treaty of Tordesillas, 76
Transportation, 82, 93, 204–205
Trinidad, 15, 17, 18, 20, 21, 166, 167, 188,
   198, 199, 200
   education, 120, 125–126
   festivals, 52, 53–59
   government, 165–173, 189–192
   illiteracy, 128
   language, 46–47
   religion, 38, 40, 42
   resources, 187, 188
   slavery, 91
   song and dance, 49–50
   unemployment, 183

Trujillo, General Rafael, 114, 157, 195
Truman, President, 164

Unemployment, 182
United Nations, 158
United States and the Americans, 27, 45,
   51, 65, 90, 93, 97–115, 125, 154–156,
   158, 159, 163–165, 181, 183, 192–195,
   196, 206
University of Havana, 108, 136, 139
University of Puerto Rico, 128, 136
University of the West Indies, 26, 137–
   139, 171
U.S.S.R., 65, 155–156

Vale Royal, 78
Vasco da Gàma, 61
Vásquez, General Horatio, 114
Venezuela, 21, 187
Village life, 91, 179
Virgin Islands, 20, 97, 203
Voodoo (Vodun), 40, 41, 42, 43, 160

Walcott, Derek, 33
War, 78–81, 94, 98, 100, 102–103, 106
War of Jenkins' Ear, 80
Warner, Thomas, 71
West Indies Federation, 170–173
Wilberforce, William, 89
Willemstad, 38, 74, 119
Williams, Eric, 94, 125, 170
Wilson, President, 107
Windward Islands, 19, 67, 168, 173
Wood, Major E. P., 172
World War I, 114
World War II, 118, 120, 125, 135
Writers, 15, 30, 32–33, 57, 58–59, 85, 91,
   94, 135, 141, 142, 143–144, 145, 147,
   148, 167

Yoruba, 39, 82
Youth, 130–131

Zayas, President, 108

About the Author

"I go walking, walking; always walking to the rhythm of things and people," says Wilfred Cartey. Born in Trinidad, Dr. Cartey's "walking" has taken him on extensive travels through Europe, North and South America, and throughout the Caribbean Islands. His most exciting trip, at the age of 13, was to the backlands of Guyana. At the age of 16 he went to Martinique as guest of the prefect of the Island as the result of winning second prize in an essay competition sponsored by Alliance Française.

Dr. Cartey's early education combined the exploration of his immediate world—running, walking, and cycling through the fields and gardens of his island—with exploration of the larger world in school. At age 11 he won a government scholarship to Queen's Royal College, the secondary school which he attended from 1943 to 1950. While there he won third prize in a worldwide essay competition and prizes in French and Spanish.

In 1951 Dr. Cartey entered the University of the West Indies on an Open West Indian University Scholarship. After graduation from UWI, a Fulbright Travel Grant brought him to Columbia University where, while completing his graduate degrees, he also taught Spanish language and literature. Since 1963 he has been teaching African literature at Columbia, in addition to presenting regular Peace Corps lectures on African and Caribbean culture, filming TV shows, and lecturing at universities across the nation. He has published several articles and has two books currently in progress.

His love for the islands has not diminished during his stay in the United States, and he keeps himself aware of current developments through contact with islanders visiting the U.S., through extensive reading, and by occasional visits to these "islands in the sun."

World Neighbors

Written to introduce young adults to their contemporaries in other lands, these books are well-documented, revealing presentations of our world neighbors. Based on firsthand knowledge of the country and illustrated with unusual photographs, the text is informal and inviting. Geographical, historical, and cultural data are woven unobtrusively into accounts of daily life. Maps, working index, chronology, and bibliography are useful additions.

ALASKA Pioneer State, by Norma Spring

BRAZIL Awakening Giant, by Kathleen Seegers

CANADA Young Giant of the North, by Adelaide Leitch

CENTRAL AMERICA Lands Seeking Unity, by Charles Paul May

CHINA AND THE CHINESE, by Lyn Harrington

EQUATORIAL AFRICA New World of Tomorrow, by Glenn Kittler

GREECE & THE GREEKS, by Lyn Harrington

INDIA Land of Rivers, by L. Winifred Bryce

ISRAEL New People in an Old Land, by Lily Edelman

JAPAN Crossroads of East and West, by Ruth Kirk

MEXICO Land of Hidden Treasure, by Ellis Credle

THE SOVIET UNION A View from Within, by Franklin Folsom

THE UNITED KINGDOM A New Britain, by Marian Moore

THE WEST INDIES Islands in the Sun, by Wilfred Cartey